Signs and Strategies for Educating Students with Brain Injuries:

A Practical Guide for Teachers and Schools

Gary Wolcott, M.Ed.

Marilyn Lash, M.S.W.

Sue Pearson, M.A.

Developed by
Research and Training Center in Rehabilitation and Childhood Trauma

Department of Physical Medicine and Rehabilitation Medicine
New England Medical Center and Tufts University School of Medicine
750 Washington St, #75K-R, Boston, MA 02111

The project was developed and supported by award # H133B30044 from
the National Institute on Disability and Rehabilitation , U.S. Department of Education.

Published by HDI Publishers
Publishers of Literature on Brain Injury
P.O. Box 131401, Houston, TX 77219
1-800-321-7037
713-682-8700
Fax 713-956-2288

August 1995

Library of Congress Cataloging-in-Publication Data

Wolcott, Gary F.
    Signs and Strategies for Educating Students with Brain Injuries: A Practical Guide
for Teachers and Schools / Gary Wolcott, Marilyn Lash, Sue Pearson.
        p.   cm.
    "Developed by Research Training Center in Rehabilitation and Childhood Trauma,
Department of Physical Medicine and Rehabilitation Medicine, New England
Medical Center and Tufts University School of Medicine."
    "The project was developed and supported by award #H133B30044 from the
National Institute on Disability and Rehabilitation, U.S. Department of Education."
    "July 1995."
    Includes bibliographical references (p.   )
    ISBN 1-882855-33-7 (alk. paper)
    1. Brain-damaged children—Education—United States   I. Lash, Marilyn.
II. Pearson, Sue, M.A.   III. Research and Training Center in Rehabilitation and
Childhood Trauma.   IV. Title.
LC4596.w65   1995
371.91'6'0973—dc20   95-34228
                                                        CIP

Contents

Acknowledgments

The development of this guide for teachers and schools is the result of collaborative efforts over several years with educators, parents, and children with brain injuries. The authors wish to thank all those who had a part in this project.

The core of this manual was developed by the authors under a grant from the Massachusetts Department of Education to the FLLAC Collaborative in Central Massachusetts. Christiane Scarpino, TBI Grant Coordinator, the educators, parents, and students provided the real world challenges that have kept this work grounded and practically focused.

Special thanks must be extended to Sue Pearson, Statewide TBI Coordinator for the State of Iowa for her writing, guidance and support.

Dr. Dennis Russo, Karen Bennett, and the entire school staff of the May Institute's program for children and adolescents with brain injuries provided very helpful feedback and guidance on the draft manuscript.

The authors are deeply indebted to those educators and parents who reviewed the draft manuscript and made suggestions for revisions and improvements. Special thanks to the following people who provided in-depth reviews:

Claire Ashley: Parent from New Hampshire

Roberta De Pompei, Ph.D.: Speech and Language Pathologist, University of Akron, Akron, OH

Kathy Gray: Vermont Achievement Center, Rutland, VT

Dr. Dick Guare: Neuropsychologist, Center for Learning and Attention Disorders, Portsmouth, NH

Elke Overton: Educator from Iowa

Dr. Brad Ross: Neuropsychologist, New England Medical Center, Boston

Dr. Ron Savage: Psychologist, May Center for Education and Neurorehabilitation, Randolph, MA

Janice Williams: Social Worker, Atlanta Rehabilitation Institute, Georgia

Beth Urbanczyk: Speech and Language Pathologist, Midwest Rehabilitation Center - Waterford, WI

About the Authors

Gary Wolcott, M.Ed.

An experienced counselor, administrator and trainer, Wolcott has long been an advocate for families of children with brain injuries as well as a trainer and consultant with school systems. He was instrumental in raising the national awareness of rehabilitation professionals and educators about the long-term cognitive effects of brain injuries in children and their impact on learning. He has been the Director of Education for the National Head Injury Foundation, founded a management and training consulting business, worked as a researcher and educational specialist at the Research and Training Center in Rehabilitation and Childhood Trauma at Tufts-New England Medical Center in Boston, and is now developing a community based transition program for young adults in Portland, Maine. As co-editor with Dr. Ron Savage, of the text *Educational Dimensoins of Acquired Brain Injury*, he has integrated clinical knowledge, research data and practical tools into a comprehensive work. Wolcott brings a pragmatic approach to the dilemmas experienced throughout the educational process by teachers, schools, families and children with acquired brain injuries that is based on professional and personal experience.

Marilyn Lash, M.S.W.

Trained as a clinical social worker, Lash became involved in program development because of the contrast between the array of medical and rehabilitation services available in hospital settings and the dearth of psychosocial and educational resources in the community. In her work as Director of Training and Principal Investigator of a research project at the Research and Training Center in Rehabilitation and Childhood Trauma at Tufts-New England Medical Center, she has focused on family and community systems. Recognizing the need of families for practical information, she has written a series of guides on the emotional impact of injuries that are published by Exceptional Parent. The guide *When your child goes to school after an injury* helps prepare families for the initial transition from the hospital to the child's local school.

An Assistant Clinical Professor in the Department of Physical Medical and Rehabilitation at Tufts University School of Medicine, Lash has written and taught extensively on the psychosocial consequences of injuries among children and the impact on families. She is Co-Chair of the Task Force on Children and Adolescents of the National Head Injury Foundation. Her involvement of families and educators in the development of this manual reflects a philosophy that families and schools are the long-term care providers for children with brain injuries and pivotal partners in the child's development, recovery and education.

Sue Pearson, M.A.

As the coordinator of statewide services for students with brain injuries in Iowa, Pearson has been an innovator in the development of school based programs. Trained in special education with a special interest in orthopedic disabilities and learning disabilities, she assists students who are transitioning from hospital based care to educational services in their local schools and community. Involved with 15 brain injury regional resource teams across the state, Pearson is skilled in building linkages with hospital and rehabilitation personnel, educational professionals and families. Building on her work in developmental disabilities for the past 20 years, she has conducted extensive training of educators and rehabilitation staff and produced two videos on school reentry and family adjustment. The joint efforts of the Iowa Department of Education, Bureau of Special Education and Iowa University Affiliated Program serve as a model for other states to recognize and meet the special educational needs of students with brain injuries. Pearson's classroom experience, consultation with teachers, and guidance of families are evident in her contribution to this manual for educators.

Understanding Educational Needs: Sorting Out the Facts

by Gary F. Wolcott, M.Ed.

and Sue Pearson, M.A.

Parents and teachers often are unfamiliar with the effects of brain injuries upon students. The needs and responses of these students are sometimes very different than those of children and youth with other disabilities. Developments in medical care, rehabilitation, and educational services within the last decade have made it possible for most children and adolescents with severe disabilities due to brain injuries to return home and go to school. Likewise, individuals with mild brain injuries, who were once assumed to be okay, are now known to be at risk for educational and behavioral difficulties. It is vital that the unique changes resulting from traumatic brain injuries be understood by each person in the student's world. The following misunderstandings often create barriers to effective educational and supportive services for students.

Myth   *The student has made a good physical recovery from an injury; therefore, he must be OK!*

Fact   Unlike a student with a visible disability, the student with a brain injury may show no outward signs of disability. Common problems like difficulty with short-term memory, inability to focus attention, or trouble following directions are not as readily obvious as physical changes such as difficulty walking or loss of speech. Because of the brain's complexity, no two injuries are the same. Even minor changes in the brain can dramatically affect a student's abilities.

What to do   Carefully observe the student's social behavior, classroom performance and ability to do age-appropriate tasks. Educators, psychologists, and rehabilitation therapists, who have training and experience evaluating children and adolescents who have had brain injuries, can identify injury-related problems in learning and behavior. Parents can help by describing changes in their child since the injury. Develop an individualized educational plan based on the unique strengths and needs of the student.

Steve sustained a brain injury at age 6 when he was struck by a motor vehicle while playing on the sidewalk. Initially, he could not recall the names for many common objects and did not recognize members of his family. Within a few weeks, however, these abilities improved and Steve's physical recovery was quite good.

His teacher and parents were surprised when he began having difficulty with what seemed to be simple tasks at home and at school. Once an easy-going child, he now had frequent temper outbursts and sometimes became physically aggressive. His reading skills were relatively good, but his comprehension was poor, which resulted in problems with his written work. The changes in Steve's behavior were attributed to his overdependence on others for assistance during his lengthy hospital stay. As a result, a behavior management program was developed — but failed to improve Steve's performance or behavior.

In reality, although Steve's physical recovery was excellent, his cognitive recovery was not. Impairment of his memory had made it difficult to learn at school, and to remember instructions/directions at home. When this was interpreted as misbehavior, it caused Steve considerable frustration. Once Steve's problems were accurately diagnosed by a pediatric neuropsychologist, adaptations for reading comprehension were made and special assistance (including a buddy system) were provided. Adjusted expectations at home and school allowed Steve to be more successful, and positive changes in his behavior were noted.

Myth	*The student with a severe brain injury will always be seriously disabled!*
Fact	The severity of the student's brain injury does not necessarily predict what the long term outcome will be. Recovery from a brain injury is not the same as the "broken bone" model. A simple fracture is likely to heal more quickly and with less long term complications than a complex fracture. Injuries to the brain don't always follow this pattern. Injury to the same part of the brain in two different students may result in two different courses of recovery. Many children and adolescents have severe injuries, yet recover with few or no long term disabilities. On the other hand, some students with mild injuries may have significant problems with thinking, memory, or controlling their behavior that result in lifelong disabilities.
What to Do	Learn as much as you can from parents, hospital and rehabilitation experts about the student's injuries and recovery. Information about the student's pre-injury performance can help identify current strengths and needs. When possible, speak directly with the medical and rehabilitation team that cared for the student. Gather enough information and records to develop a complete picture of the student's needs and strengths. Base the student's educational program on identified strengths and needs, not on the severity of the initial injury.

A motor vehicle crash involving two cars left Maryann with a severe brain injury. After she emerged from coma, her memory was impaired and she became frustrated when she was unable to recall the names for everyday objects. Her social skills were frequently inappropriate and she made offensive comments to friends. Previously a talented pianist, she now had difficulty playing simple music. Maryann, like many individuals, showed a great deal of improvement during the first 1–2 years after her accident. However, her circle of friends decreased significantly. She continued to have difficulty with academic work and abandoned her music altogether.

Several years later, Maryann and her parents continue to notice small improvements in all areas. They feel, as do her teachers, that a structured social skills group and a few special friends have helped her re-learn some critical skills and her social life is improving. They have also seen her interest in the piano return and, gradually, she has been able to deal with more difficult music and techniques. Although her rate of progress is not as rapid as it was initially, Maryann, her parents and her teachers continue to see steady improvement in many areas of her life.

Myth   *The student with a mild traumatic brain injury will have no problems recovering!*

Fact   Violent shaking or a blow to the head, even without loss of consciousness, can cause a brain injury that results in serious long-term problems with thinking, memory, and behavior control. It is vital that no assumptions be made about a student's level of disability. A student with a mild traumatic brain injury may have subtle problems that go unrecognized, especially if the student was not hospitalized.

The family physician or emergency room doctor may indicate that the student is medically OK, but the student may notice unexplained difficulties. Headaches, difficulty concentrating, mood swings, a "feeling of not being myself," may be indicators of a brain injury that need to be evaluated by a specialist with experience in mild traumatic brain injuries. Some students with mild brain injuries have reported that they were afraid they were "going crazy" so they told no one about their symptoms.

What to do   Assure the student that there is a reason for these difficulties. Refer the student and parents to a physician familiar with the effects of traumatic brain injuries. A neuropsychological evaluation may also help define subtle learning and thinking problems and identify educational and behavioral strategies to help the student.

Jeff's brain injury went undiagnosed for almost a year after his injury. Jeff was involved in a car/pedestrian collision when he was 8 years old. Although he did not lose consciousness, medical reports describe him as being "unresponsive" immediately following the crash and "disoriented" for a few days afterward. Jeff had several broken bones and this prevented him from returning to school for several months. While convalescing at home, a tutor was provided by the school so that he would not fall behind in his work.

He began having academic and behavior problems almost immediately after he returned to school. Everyone felt that he "just needed a little more time" to adjust to school. Jeff continued to fail at things that had previously been easy for him, and seemed unable to focus his attention for any length of time. Furthermore, his mother became concerned about his frequent headaches and what appeared to be depression. Jeff confided that he often felt like crying, but didn't understand why. A year after his injury, a medical evaluation found that Jeff's brain injury was probably more significant than thought initially. Medication was prescribed for his depression and attention problems, and school curriculum adjustments were made. Jeff is no longer blamed for problems beyond his control.

Myth	*The younger the student is when injured, the better the recovery!*
Fact	The brain's ability to "rewire" itself is more limited than once thought. Medical care and rehabilitation programs can not repair damage to the brain. The rehabilitation process focuses on using the student's strengths and abilities to make up for the loss of others.
	While previously learned skills are often left largely intact after a brain injury, acquiring new skills is a common problem. When a child is injured at a young age, fewer basic living and educational skills have been acquired than in an older child. Lacking this foundation, the child cannot draw on previously mastered skills to compensate for changes caused by an injury. Finding ways to help a younger child adjust can be much more difficult than for a teenager or adult with more life experience.
What to Do	Early intervention is vital for a younger student who has had a brain injury. Regular evaluation by developmental specialists who are experienced in brain injury can identify problems that might be overlooked in a pre-school setting. An early intervention program can help the student build critical skills for later school years.

Mary fell off of a tractor while visiting her uncle's farm when she was 3 years of age. Her brain injury was severe and resulted in cognitive impairments and paralysis of her left side. Mary was injured prior to learning how to independently care for herself and the acquired cognitive and physical impairments made feeding and dressing difficult for her. Since she had not had any previous experience with reading and math, academic activities were also challenging. She was fortunate in that she had attended a pre-school for children with special needs and the teacher had identified several helpful strategies and adaptations for her physical and cognitive problems. This information was communicated to her kindergarten teacher who was able to provide similar assistance — which resulted in a good transition into the new classroom.

Myth   *After seven or eight months, a student with a brain injury will not improve anymore because the brain's repair mechanisms have shut down.*

Fact   There is no timetable for recovery. Rapid changes occur most often in the first seven to eight months after an injury. Progress can continue for months and years. It may be slower, and new difficulties may appear as the student develops and attempts more complex tasks, but progress can continue indefinitely.

What to do   There are no sure predictors of long term outcome. Predictions can even create a barrier for the student and discourage educators and families. Focus on where the student is today and what steps are needed in the short term. Build the student's educational plan upon the functional performance within the school environment and regular assessment by educational and allied health professionals.

Doctors did not expect Michele to live after prolonged swelling caused significant damage to her brain. Everyone, including her parents, was surprised when her medical condition stabilized and she began the slow process of recovery. Her parents were told that Michele would probably not be able to walk or talk and would most likely have "no real quality of life." In reality, within a few months, Michele regained all of these skills, and soon after, returned to school. She attended regular classes, receiving specialized assistance from a classroom aide, but made little progress in academic work after several months of instruction. The teacher felt that Michele's parents were "in denial" when they insisted that she be maintained in the regular classroom and that she receive extended year programming. The parents hired a tutor during the summer months to give her a more individualized approach to academic work and after approximately 6 months, Michele began to make steady progress in reading. Not only did she begin to maintain a sight word vocabulary, but she actively looked for books at the public library that were within her ability range. Michele's most significant progress in reading occurred almost two years after her injury.

Myth	*A brain injury erases your memory!*
Fact	Usually a student with a brain injury will retain most previous learning and knowledge. Difficulty learning new information is a more common problem. Sometimes a student will have post-traumatic amnesia, which is the inability to recall events just before and after the injury. Or a student might experience gaps in memory and skills.
What to do	Work with the student to identify what memories, skills and motivators are intact. Use this information to enhance the student's educational program by building on these strengths.

Some of the student's peers may expect that their friend will not remember anything upon coming home from the hospital and returning to school. Others may be surprised at the changes they observe. Talk with the student's peers about their expectations and fears. Discuss ways that they can support their friend.

Jamie was injured in a summer bicycle collision when he was traveling at a high rate of speed and ran into a tree. He sustained a moderate brain injury but recovered in a relatively short period of time. In September, he returned to school and seemed to be doing relatively well, both socially and academically. As the semester continued, however, his teachers noticed that he began to have increased difficulty with assignments. Upon further investigation, it appeared that Jamie's initial academic success may have occurred during the first few weeks of school because the time was spent reviewing material that had been presented the year before. Like many individuals, Jamie was more successful in *re-learning* previously learned information. Once the students began working on new concepts and skills, he was less successful. Although he was able to make progress with new material, teachers found that his learning rate was slower than it had been in the past, which was frustrating for him. They found that modification of some assignments and providing additional organization and structure was helpful in terms of his success.

Myth   *Denial is bad! The student and family must face the harsh reality of a disability in order for progress to occur!*

Fact   Denial comes in many forms for many different reasons. A student's brain injury may have affected his self-awareness. The injury may limit his understanding and insight into problems. On the other hand, denial may be an emotional self-defense that is needed by the student. Denial is an expected and normal coping response. Parents and families are often accused of denial when they refuse to acknowledge their child's difficulties. Medical and educational professionals sometimes misinterpret parents' intense hopes and beliefs in their child's improvement as a denial of the disability. Parents need to hold onto this hope in order to face the unknown future.

What to do Don't try to force reality! Use the goals identified by the student or parents. Then break the goals down into small practical, educational steps that must be achieved. This allows the family and student to use time and their experience to build a more realistic view of the student's disabilities.

Denial of a disability may be damaging if parents (or children) develop unrealistic expectations that lead to repeated failure. However, all of us have ideas and dreams about things we want to be able to do and all of us have, at some point, been allowed to try and fail — which is a natural part of life and the learning process. In Justin's case, his parents felt that he was being unrealistic when he decided to return to college after experiencing a brain injury in a serious automobile crash. They recognized personality changes and memory problems and were concerned about his ability to manage his academic work and personal life. After months of family arguments, they were willing to let him try. Justin returned to school the following semester, intent on carrying a full academic load. After the first quarter, he realized that he was not able to keep up with the academic demands and decided to drop three of his classes. This allowed him to do reasonably well in the three remaining classes, although he admitted that his grades were not as good as before and he felt he was working much harder than before. Justin's parents now admit that it was a good idea to let him return to school. Although they recognize that his abilities are different now, they feel he is making good progress and see significant improvement in his self esteem.

Signs and Changes to Watch for in Students with Brain Injuries

by Marilyn Lash, M.S.W.

Introduction

In 1991, a federal amendment to the education act (P.L. 101-476, IDEA) was passed. It recognizes that students with traumatic brain injuries have serious and complex disabilities which can result in needs for special education and related services. It specifically states that students with traumatic brain injuries are not to be classified as mentally retarded, emotionally disturbed, learning disabled, or any other inappropriate category. Although many children with traumatic brain injuries appear to physically recover, studies have shown that they may have long-lasting impairments or difficulties in thinking and behavior which affect their learning, emotional and social development. The amendment states that schools are to provide these children with access and funding for the neuropsychological, speech and language, and educational evaluations that are needed for individualized education programs.

Unfortunately, many teachers have not received training about traumatic brain injuries. This places them in a very difficult position when children enter or return to school after an injury. This section was written to help school staff, especially teachers, prepare and problem solve as they identify, teach and coordinate educational programs for students with traumatic brain injuries. Teachers are the experts in education, not rehabilitation professionals who largely work in health care settings. The information presented here is intended to help bridge the gap between hospitals and schools. Its goal is to help teachers understand how a brain injury can affect a student's abilities and performance at school.

There are many unknowns about the immediate and long-term effects of brain injuries to children. This area simply has not been well researched. By contrast, much more is known about children with other developmental disabilities such as mental retardation, autism, or learning disabilities.

Many children did not survive their injuries until recently due to advances in emergency medical services, neurosurgery, acute care and rehabilitation. Among survivors, the relationship between the brain injury and the child's educational needs has often been overlooked or misunderstood. This was no fault of the school or teacher; the information simply has not been available.

Inadequate communication between hospitals, rehabilitation programs and schools has frequently made the school's job even harder. Very few health care professionals have more than a superficial understanding of what is meant by "special education." They often make many inaccurate assumptions about the resources, programs and funds that schools have available for children with special educational needs.

Student Recovery

A student's recovery from a brain injury is hard to predict. Each injury is different and much depends on the areas of the brain that are affected. Academic skills and knowledge acquired before the injury can affect future performance. The age of the student when injured is also a factor since a child's brain continues to develop and organize through adolescence. When injuries interrupt "normal" developmental patterns and milestones, the effects on subsequent stages are largely unknown. Some difficulties do not appear for months or years after an injury. They often become apparent as the student's development requires more complex and challenging tasks and processes. Many times, young children have excellent physical recoveries. This appearance of well-being may be deceptive however. More subtle cognitive, emotional and behavioral changes from the injury may be unidentified and their symptoms misinterpreted. All these factors are cause for families and teachers to work together as students with brain injuries return to school.

Changes to watch for when a student has a brain injury

The educational plan is a flexible guide that must continually change as students progress and recover from brain injuries. Goals, abilities, and difficulties change for all children as they grow. Learning is a continual process that is never complete for any individual. For children who have had traumatic brain injuries, this process will be more complex. It may have different effects at various stages of the child's education. As the complexity of learning increases as the student advances through grades, different abilities and skills will be required.

It is most important that parents, educators and rehabilitation specialists work as a team with these students. Teachers are in critical positions to influence chances for success in school. Depending on the school and classroom, the teacher may be with the student from one to six hours a day. This gives the teacher a unique opportunity to assess the student's abilities as well as difficulties. It also places a major responsibility on the teacher to determine how the brain injury has affected the student and to determine how to help this student learn. This is not an easy challenge.

Medical and rehabilitation professionals have only a very limited understanding of how brain injuries affect the child's ability to learn. All too often teachers are given the responsibility for a student's education after a brain injury without much preparation or information. Families who are accustomed to the intensive and individualized services of rehabilitation and hospital-based programs often have expectations that schools cannot meet. Teachers must simultaneously juggle the special needs of many students in the classroom.

It is important for hospital and school staff to help families understand the differences between hospital and school based programs. Teachers usually do not have the time or resources to give separate and intensive instruction and attention to the student as was done by therapists and specialists in rehabilitation programs. Less intensive therapy services in schools are frequently misinterpreted by families as inadequate. In fact, they may be an indication of the student's progress to a later stage of recovery where less intensive services are needed.

Schools often ask psychologists to test the intelligence of children being evaluated for special education to determine their academic levels. It is very important that children with traumatic brain injuries be evaluated from a neuropsychological approach. This method looks at the different functions of the brain, including skills required for organizing, processing and recalling information. It identifies *how* the brain injury has affected the student's ability to learn, not simply what the student has learned in the past.

Many of the emotions, behaviors and reactions that children experience after a brain injury cause problems for children at school because they are not recognized or are misunderstood. These symptoms are listed with suggestions to help teachers identify patterns, develop strategies for the classroom, and improve the student's ability to learn.

Summary of common changes in students who have had brain injuries

- Tiredness and fatigue

- Irritability, angry outbursts, impulsivity

- Aggressive acting out or misbehaving

- Passive behavior

- Depression

- Social immaturity

- Sexually inappropriate behavior

- Forgetfulness

- Distractibility

- Difficulty following directions

- Poor organizational skills

- Poor or lower grades

Tiredness and Fatigue

School Signs

A student looks pale and drawn, complains of being tired, frequently yawns, tunes out, or even dozes off during class. The student stops to rest in midst of activities, especially those requiring physical energy or intense concentration.

Questions for teachers to ask

- Does this happen at certain times each day?
- Is the student more alert in the morning or the afternoon?
- Does it occur more often during the beginning, middle or end of the week?
- How long has it been since the student was released from the hospital?
- Is a full school day too tiring for this student?
- Should the school day be shortened?
- Should breaks or rest periods be provided during the school day?
- Are there schedule changes that will allow for easier pacing?
- Is the student receiving medications that might affect attention and energy level?
- Can school attendance or assignments be better coordinated with hours of alertness?

Questions to ask parents

- Does the student take any medications that might cause sleepiness or lowered energy?
- Has there been a change in the dose or schedule of medications?
- Have parents noticed any tiredness or fatigue? When and how often?
- How is the student's energy and fatigue on the weekends?
- What is the student's sleep pattern at home? Too little sleep? Trouble waking up? Sleep problems?

Example:	Susan was hospitalized for 17 weeks after being hit by a car while riding her bicycle. When she went home, she still tired easily and napped each afternoon. It was 8 more weeks before she returned to school. During this time a tutor came to her home daily for 2 hours. When she returned to school full time, her teachers noted that she looked tired and pale by mid week. Frequently she chose to remain in her homeroom during recess. During study periods, she often laid her head on her desk and took short naps.
Intervention:	Despite the appearance of physical well-being, Susan simply had not regained her physical stamina and endurance. Arrangements were made to shorten her school day for the next three months. She returned home for lunch, had a short nap or rest period and then finished her school work with a home tutor for one and a half hours. Over the next four months, her time at school gradually increased, but she never had the same stamina as before her injury.

Irritability, Angry Outbursts, Impulsivity

School signs

The student becomes irritable, short-tempered or abrupt, especially when noise and activity levels increase or in stressful situations.

This may be directly due to damage to the brain, or it may be an emotional reaction to the injury or a combination. A neuropsychological evaluation and testing can sort this out by identifying damaged areas of the brain and their functions. Be sure to ask for specific recommendations that either will help the student control this behavior or will change the environment or tasks to establish a better "fit" with the student's current skills.

Questions to ask

- Is the student aware of this behavior?
- Does noise and activity affect the student's behavior?
- Is this behavior more common in unstructured areas such as the playground or hallways?
- Does it happen more often during certain activities or with particular classmates?
- Can you identify activities that precede and follow this behavior or outburst? Try tracking them for 1–2 weeks to see if there is any pattern.
- Does this student have a lot of "catching up" to do in school work? Is the student feeling overwhelmed by this?
- How many classes are taken and is this too much for now? Is there a particular time of day or stage of the week when these behaviors increase or lessen?

Example   Tom's quick temper was a constant source of irritation to his teacher. She never knew when he was going to explode when she corrected him for errors in class. He frequently threw his papers on the floor or accused the teacher of picking on him unfairly.

Intervention   The teacher kept a record of these temper outbursts for 2 weeks and noted that they happened most often during math class. Although he was getting passing grades on his written home-work, he had trouble completing math problems on the black-board during class exercises. With the added pressure of his classmates observing, Tom couldn't concentrate to follow instructions. He became embarrassed when he made mistakes and then got angry. The teacher figured out that Tom had trouble following verbal instructions for blackboard exercises. When instructions were written down for him, his errors de-creased and so did his angry outbursts.

Aggressive "acting out" or misbehaving

School signs

The student frequently hits others, swears, is rude, gets into arguments and disobeys rules.

This behavior needs immediate attention because it quickly can result in punishment by teachers and loss of friends. It is especially important that both the family and school staff discuss the relationship of the brain injury and the behavior with a neuropsychologist. Too often, a student is mistakenly labeled as a troublemaker at school and punished when the underlying problem is difficulty in controlling aggressions and actions due to a brain injury. This can compound a student's feelings of lowered self-esteem and the belief that, "I can't do anything right." It can lead to serious depression.

Questions to ask

■ Did the student show any of these behaviors before the injury?

■ Does this disrupt the class and disturb others? How do teachers and classmates respond?

■ Does this happen more often with certain teachers or peers?

■ Do these behaviors occur more often inside or outside the classroom?

■ How much individual attention does this student get at school?

■ Does a smaller, more structured setting decrease these behaviors?

■ Does this happen at certain times? During transitions or changes in the routine?

Questions to ask parents

■ Does this happen at home? When, how often and how do parents respond to it?

■ Is the student on any medication that might be a factor? Does it need to be increased, decreased, eliminated or changed?

Example   Peter was being sent to the middle school principal's office constantly for punching or hitting classmates. While he had never been the perfect student before his injury, now he was quickly gaining the reputation of troublemaker. No amount of detention or warnings were doing any good. Peter was unable to give any reasons for his increasingly frequent fights. A guidance counselor noted that episodes happened most often in the hallways, during gym classes and on the school bus. Settings with large amounts of noise and activity seemed to trigger him quickly.

Intervention   Consultation with the neuropsychologist revealed that since his brain injury, Peter quickly became overwhelmed in group situations particularly when noise and activity levels were high. When pushed or shoved in the crowded hallway or school bus, he responded by kicking or punching. Arrangements were made for Peter to change classes five minutes ahead of schedule to minimize time in crowded hallways. The school bus driver reserved a front seat for him. Setting up this structure helped decrease the noise, crowds and confusion that Peter had trouble handling. This helped him feel more in control and fights became less frequent.

Passive behavior

School signs

The student "doesn't start anything on his own," or just sits there, "staring off into space." Unmotivated and lazy are words that have been used to describe this student. As this student is quiet, problems may not be noticed readily. This student easily "slips through the cracks." Passive behavior can be interpreted as not caring.

The passivity may be caused by damage to areas of the brain that control initiating and planning behavior. Once this student gets started, productivity is possible but a structured pathway is needed.

Questions to ask

- What helps this student get started in an activity?
- What prompts/cues help this student when stuck midway through a task?
- Can the student complete the task once started?
- Do written or spoken prompts or cues work best?
- Is there a backup cuing system for when the teacher is unavailable?
- Would a notebook with instructions in words or pictures help? Can reminders be placed on the student's desk?
- What reinforcers can be used to encourage the student to get through the task?
- Can an incentive system be set up with built in cues or check points?

Example   Amy seemed to be constantly day dreaming in class. She listened well and was polite, but she just couldn't seem to keep herself organized. Her teacher was becoming frustrated because she had to be reminded of "every little thing" or else her homework never got done or returned to class. The medical reports noted that due to her brain injury, Amy's ability to initiate or self-prompt was severely limited. She needed cues to help her start activities, but the teacher simply didn't have the time to lead her every step of the way in a class with 23 other students.

Intervention   Amy was given a notebook with critical checkpoints. This was organized by activities where she most frequently got "stuck." For example, under the heading end of "Homework" there was a list to check for each subject; a place to write assigned pages, chapters, or problems; a section for the day and time the assignment was due; a place to check when the work was done, and a place to check that the completed work was placed in the section marked "Completed work to bring back to school".

Depression

Feelings of sadness and loss are normal reactions to a disabling injury. They may even be positive signs that the student has become aware of the changes caused by the injury and is trying to adjust. However, if a student shows or expresses a deep sense of sadness for a long time and makes statements that reflect a loss of self-worth or interest in life, then there is cause for serious concern by school staff. Any statements about death or suicide must be taken seriously.

It is important to determine the reasons for this depression, particularly to sort out the emotional and physical causes. Some medications can contribute to depression as well. A neuropsychologist or physician experienced in children with brain injuries can evaluate this and design a treatment plan. Social workers and counselors can provide valuable support and counseling. Depression can become a serious condition if ignored. A psychiatric consultation should be considered if the student isn't responding to intervention.

Questions to ask

- Is the depression related to the area of the brain that was injured?
- Does this student feel different from or "less than" his peers?
- Do friends still spend time with this student or avoid him/her?
- Were close friends or relatives killed or injured in the accident?
- Has this student talked about suicide or death?
- Does this student appear to have given up?
- Could any medications be affecting mood and emotions?
- Have eating or sleeping patterns changed?
- Are there changes or issues within the family that might be relevant?
- Does the student experience mood swings?

Example

Susan expressed little interest in her school work and was receiving lower grades in almost every subject. This was in marked contrast to her achievements prior to her injury. She avoided any involvement in school social activities or after school programs. She spent little time with her friends at school. Not knowing what to make of her behavior, her friends were at first puzzled, then felt rejected and finally began avoiding her. A referral was made to the school social worker.

Intervention

The social worker called her parents and set up an appointment to meet. Her parents admitted that they also were very worried since she kept to herself at home, shut herself in her room for hours, was eating poorly and having frequent nightmares. They revealed that Susan's older sister had been killed in the car crash. Susan's sister had just picked her up from basketball practice. The car was hit by a drunk driver just two blocks from home.

Counseling with Susan revealed that she felt responsible for her sister's death. This was reinforced by her parents' devastating grief and isolation which Susan misinterpreted as anger and rejection. This family needed months of counseling to be able to talk about their losses without feeling overwhelmed. Susan needed help to overcome feeling guilty that she had survived.

With permission, the school social worker shared the cause of Susan's depression with her teachers who gave her extra attention and support during this difficult period. An effective method teachers used to help Susan express her feelings of loss and confusion was the use of art and poetry. Teachers were especially sensitive to her desires about whether she wished to have these shared with her class and family. As she used this method to release some of the emotional tension pent up inside, teachers noted that she gradually emerged from her protective shell and withdrawal.

Social behaviors and rules

School signs

The student may show less mature behaviors than prior to the injury. Examples are constant interruptions while others are talking, inability to wait, tactless remarks, repeating words or actions like a "stuck record" and messy eating habits. This student may "miss cues" from others about what is expected and need direct instructions about what to do and how to do it. Classmates may mimic or make fun of this student because these behaviors seem "babyish." When present among adolescents, peers may find these social breaches embarrassing and reject or avoid the student. The adolescent may be seen as "weird" or a "nerd".

Questions to ask

- What is the teacher's response when these behaviors occur in class?
- How do peers react in class? How do they react outside the classroom?
- Has a neuropsychologist been asked to evaluate the cause of these behaviors and give suggestions for responses by teachers and peers?
- Are these behaviors greater or less when the student feels nervous, anxious, relaxed or tired?
- How often and when during the day do they occur?
- What responses encourage or reinforce the behaviors?
- What responses will help change the behaviors?
- Is the student aware when behaviors do not fit the situation?

Example   Tom's behaviors when he returned to school seemed more
                   typical of a 6 year old than a 3rd grader. His joke telling and
                   spitball tossing during class was especially annoying. The
                   teacher's frustration delighted his classmates, whose giggles
                   further encouraged him.

Intervention   Tom's ability to monitor his behavior and judge its appropriate-
                   ness to the situation had been damaged. He could go on end-
                   lessly and reveled in the attention it brought him. He not only
                   needed the teacher to establish limits for him by telling him
                   firmly when to stop, but he also needed the teacher's help to
                   channel his energy into other activities that were appropriate
                   for the classroom. Placing him in charge of distributing and
                   collecting special supplies, such as chalk or crayons for special
                   projects, was a more productive way of using his energy.

Sexually inappropriate behavior

School signs

Verbally or physically inappropriate sexual behaviors can be a direct result of a brain injury. This behavior can be especially upsetting and embarrassing for parents and friends of adolescents. Teachers and other students may be insulted, puzzled, or shocked by sexual comments, gestures or actions that are out of context. Parents and school staff often worry that such behaviors could lead to sexual intercourse or abuse by peers or strangers.

Possible approaches range from a behavior management program, counseling and/or psychotherapy, to medication. The student should be counseled on appropriate behaviors. Peers should also be oriented to the issues associated with brain injury and provided specific ways to support the student.

Questions to ask

- Does this behavior happen privately or in public?
- How explicit are the sexual comments and behaviors at school?
- Do they occur more often with particular individuals?
- How do family, peers and teachers respond to sexual comments, gestures/behaviors?
- Is the student aware when this behavior embarrasses others?
- How do peers interpret these behaviors?
- Can this be seen as a sexual advance by peers?

Example   When Alison returned to high school after her injury, she frequently asked male classmates for rides home, asked them for dates, and made suggestive remarks. This behavior differed from her previous shy demeanor and limited dating experience. Her friends were frequently embarrassed by her. Those who knew her prior to the accident were cautious and puzzled, but others thought she was an aggressive flirt and encouraged her. Her friends feared that she could readily get into "trouble."

Intervention   The guidance counselor met with Alison's closest friends to explain that these changed behaviors were related to her brain injury. Her closest friends became her allies and formed a buddy system while she was at school. They quietly spread the word among her peers that she was still recovering from her injury, that her suggestive remarks and behaviors were not to be treated as jokes or encouraged. The counselor also met with Alison to explain and reinforce the possible consequences of her sexual behaviors.

Forgetfulness

School signs

Memory problems and forgetfulness are common and may be temporary or long term. There are numerous aids and techniques to help including appointment books, calendars, lists of what needs to be done and the order in which to do them.

Questions to ask

- What kind of information does the student tend to forget?
- Is short-term or long-term memory more affected?
- Is it a problem of receiving new information or retrieving already learned information?
- Are there particular kinds of information that are most often forgotten, such as places, names, activities, events or dates?
- How does stress, excitement or fatigue affect memory?
- What type of cueing or reminders compensate for memory difficulties?
- Is punctuality a problem?
- Does the student have difficulty remembering the location of classes, teacher names, and homework assignments?

Example   Bruce's forgetfulness at school was constantly resulting in mix-ups and tardiness. Some days were worse than others.

Intervention   Bruce was given a looseleaf notebook as a recorder and prompter. There were sections set up for each day, week and month. At the beginning of each day, he reviewed his daily schedule with his homeroom teacher. It identified any special activities, assignments or events for that day, including the time, place and person in charge. Whenever he became mixed up or confused, he referred to his notebook. The teacher made sure that he wrote down all homework assignments or special requests. Changes in schedule, messages for his parents, and special requests were recorded. Due dates for items such as lunch money, recreational school trips, or special events were all listed. A checklist was included for the end of each day to insure that all materials were gathered for the evening's homework assignments before leaving school. An extra set of textbooks was provided for home so that he did not have to remember to carry his books back and forth to school.

Distractibility

School signs

The student's assignments are often incomplete. Many tasks are started but rarely finished. Noise and attention easily interrupt the student's concentration. Changes in the physical arrangement of the classroom, a quieter space to work, and shortened assignments may help.

Questions to ask

- How many other students are in the classroom?
- Does the class size affect the student's ability to concentrate?
- How long can the student focus on an activity without becoming distracted?
- What helps this student concentrate? Would an aide or tutor help?
- Can assignments be broken into shorter tasks?
- How near the window or door does the student sit?
- Are distractions readily seen or heard?
- Have other seating arrangements been tried?
- Does distractibility increase when the student is tired or during particular sections of the school day?
- Is quantity of work being emphasized over acquiring the skill or concept?
- Should behavior plans or medication consultations be considered?

Example   Mary simply couldn't seem to concentrate long enough to finish anything in class. She understood the instructions and was capable of doing the work, but it just didn't get done most of the time.

Intervention   By moving her seat from the outside row near the corridor to the center and closer to the teacher, Mary was less distracted by noise and activity and better able to concentrate.

Cannot follow directions

School signs

Students with brain injuries often have trouble completing tasks when more than two directions are given. For example: "Take out your math book, open to page 83, and do problems 1–20." The student may get the math book out, but not know what to do next. One suggestion is for the teachers to write down the steps, either on the blackboard or an individual assignment sheet at the student's desk. A classmate may be assigned to give prompts if the teacher is unavailable.

Questions to ask

■ Is the problem mainly in following directions?

■ How many steps of directions can the student follow?

■ Does the student have trouble figuring out the order to do things?

■ Can the student keep up with the regular class assignments or do they need to be modified?

■ Does the student follow directions better in one mode or another: visually, written, auditory, physical?

Example	No matter how hard he tried, Kevin got mixed up when the teacher gave instructions unless they were written down. As a result, his work was often incomplete or filled with errors. While others were busy working, Kevin was still trying to sort out the instructions and usually ran out of time. As a result, he was close to failing many subjects.
Intervention	The teacher set up a signal with Kevin that meant he was to wait before starting the exercise. The teacher then broke down the instructions into several mini steps and wrote them down for him to follow. He was given extra time to finish since others started ahead of him.

Poor Organizational Skills

School signs

The student finds it hard to organize information, cannot figure out the correct order to do things, or can't do more than one thing at a time. The student is often late getting places. Homework or class assignments are often late or not even started. These are signs of difficulty with problem solving and planning for the future.

Questions to ask

■ Does the student have a written plan for each school day?

■ How do teachers give instructions?

■ Does the student need a written step-by-step plan for assignments?

■ Does the student have a "buddy" at school who can help when a teacher is not available?

■ Have you explained the organizational methods used with the student in the classroom to parents so that they can use the same methods at home when helping with assignments?

■ Does the student seem to understand details but have difficulty with the overall concept or does the student understand the big picture but miss the details?

Example   Jane had several different teachers and moved to 4 different classrooms each day. While she did very well in some subjects, in others she was failing miserably. This inconsistency puzzled her teachers.

Intervention   Many of the techniques already discussed such as written schedules, broken-down instructions, and environmental changes were being used by several teachers and were effective in helping Jane organize her work. However, not all her teachers were using the same, if any, methods. Not only did Jane have to change classes and teachers several times a day, but she also had to try to adjust to different methods of instruction and learning. Some teachers gave written directons, others did it verbally. In some classes, she got help from friends, while in others she was on her own. Some classes required oral reports, others used timed tests and still others assigned written essays.

Puzzled by the fluctuations in her abilities in different classes, she was referred to the school psychologist, who reviewed her medical records, testing reports, and then talked with each of her teachers. A weekly meeting was set up with all of her teachers to plan a consistent approach. This coordination made a big difference in her classroom performance and ability to complete her work. Soon it was reduced to a meeting every two weeks and eventually monthly. Jane's frustration decreased and her work became more consistent across classes, although she still had more difficulty in some subjects than others.

Poor grades

School signs

The student's grades are lower than before the injury. Certain subjects are now more difficult. Parents, classmates and teachers make comments such as, "He's just being lazy" or "She's not really trying." Standard intelligence and educational testing can be misleading when scores are "normal" after a brain injury. When students can not do class work at this "normal" level, they may be considered lazy or unmotivated. This can add to a student's feeling of failure and parents' disappointment.

It is important for any evaluations to focus on the learning process after an injury, not simply what information remains stored in the student's memory. This is especially true of students who were above average prior to their injury who can "coast" on old learning until they are confronted with unfamiliar concepts.

Questions to ask

- Has a neuropsychological evaluation been completed with this student since the injury and how long ago?

- Is the school using information from intelligence or educational testing that was done prior to the student's injury?

- If the school has repeated this testing, is it now an accurate test to determine changes that may have resulted from a brain injury?

- What are the credentials of the professional who evaluated and tested the student and what experience does that person have with brain injuries?

- Did the testing reports give concrete and practical suggestions for teachers to help the student learn at school?

- Do reports and recommendations discuss strengths as well as weaknesses?

- Have all medical terms been explained to school staff?

Example   Tom's grades slipped from a solid B+ average to C. The psychologist's report offered no insight into this, as standard testing showed abilities well above average. His grades were particularly puzzling because Tom clearly excelled in some subjects and in others he just seemed hopelessly lost. He followed instructions in class, asked good questions, and did his homework. On multiple choice test questions he scored high; however, on essay questions he rambled on with no clear logic or order. He seemed to concentrate on just writing down as much information as he could remember and hoped that some of it answered the question.

Intervention   Any major change or inconsistency in grades following an injury is a sign that difficulties may be related to changes in how the brain functions. Tom's recall and recognition of information was good. This is why he did well on multiple choice tests. It was his ability to conceptualize and draw relationships between cause and effect and to organize information that was damaged; hence, his difficulty with essay tests. By modifying test formats to give him more structured questions, his grades improved.

Classroom Strategies: Responding to Student Changes

by Sue Pearson, M.A.

Parents describe a variety of changes and adjustments after their child has sustained a brain injury. But when asked about the long term challenges they face as a family, school re-entry is frequently at the top of the list. Although some children can recover from brain injuries with few or no apparent problems, others may return to school with different abilities and personality changes. This can be puzzling and sometimes frustrating to students in the classroom and to the teacher if careful preparation and planning are not done prior to the student's return. This preparation should include educating the students and the teacher about brain injury.

Most teachers have received little, if any, instruction about brain injury in their course work and may feel overwhelmed and unsure of what to expect. Inappropriate expectations for these students can lead to behavior problems and disruption for the entire classroom. After experiencing a frustrating day at school, the student may have less tolerance for the everyday activities at home and may take out pent-up frustrations on family members. Many parents report that their children seem overly fatigued and frustrated when they arrive home from school and are less able to cope with family life. This can result in family life being disrupted even more.

This chapter was written to help teachers and other school staff identify the common changes and difficulties that students experience after brain injury and provides suggestions for dealing with these problems.

Frontal lobe

The medical literature tells us that when a child sustains a brain injury, there is usually damage to the frontal and temporal lobe areas of the brain — simply because of their location and the way the skull is constructed in these regions. The frontal lobe of the brain is responsible for "executive functions," which include inhibiting responses or reactions, initiating responses/reactions and using good judgment and reasoning. It is also responsible for organization and is involved in focusing attention. The frontal lobe "governs" much of what we do and helps us make decisions about our actions.

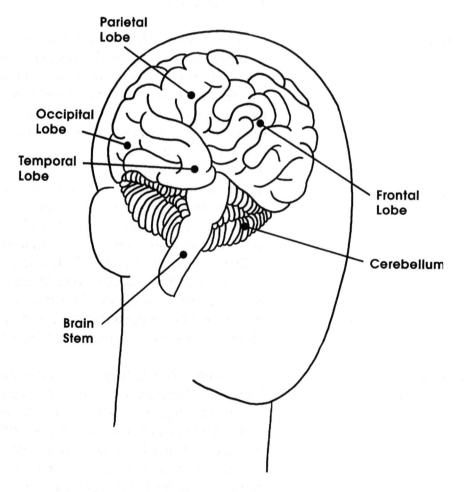

Temporal lobe

The temporal lobe is associated with the concept of time and is also involved with emotion, memory and hearing. When the frontal and temporal lobe areas of the brain are injured, it is not surprising to see students who have difficulty with:

- attention
- organization and memory
- hearing
- initiating conversation, activities or assignments
- controlling moods

Occipital lobe

The occipital lobe, located in the back of the head, is responsible primarily for vision. When a person receives a blow to the front of the head (frontal lobe) there can be an opposing force, or contre coup, to the back of the head (occipital lobe), even though the person did not sustain an "outside" injury to that area. An injury to the occipital area may result in damage to the optic nerve and may affect vision.

Parietal lobe

The parietal lobe of the brain is involved with touch perception and sensation. Children with damage to this area of the brain may not be able to perceive when they are being touched or when they are touching something or someone. It would, for example, be difficult for a child to play an instrument like the violin or piano without watching his/her fingers. Similarly, this same child might have difficulty with keyboarding/typing. Another example of difficulty would be a student reaching into a bag or purse, trying to identify a set of keys, a comb or a tube of lipstick by touch alone.

Left and right hemispheres

Students with damage to the left hemisphere of the brain may have more difficulty with language related activities, such as reading and writing, whereas a person with right hemisphere damage may have more difficulty with spatial skills and social perceptions (i.e., reading body language, facial expressions). And yet, no one area of the brain works in isolation from the others; they are connected in countless ways, many of which are yet unknown.

Effects upon students and importance of teachers

Based on experience, we know that students with brain injuries may have difficulty expressing what they know because of language and/or organizational problems. We also know that these students fatigue more easily, and often do not have the stamina for a full school day after an extended hospital stay. We suspect that they may be working/concentrating much harder to do things that they used to do quite easily which can also increase fatigue.

Transitions from one activity to another might also require more preparation. Individuals with brain injuries may have difficulty dealing with abrupt changes in a routine or schedule. Brain injury survivors tell us that structure and organization are key elements to their success and independence. When the routine is changed, they may experience confusion and find themselves less able to cope and function, which can be unsettling, to say the least. Imagine losing your daily planner or the calendar that lists all your future appointments and meetings!

When a person has a brain injury, it is unlikely that just one area of the brain has sustained injury. Teachers must be aware of the many possible effects on a student's learning, social interactions and overall behavior in the classroom. As a result of I.D.E.A., more children with special needs are being served in the "least restrictive environment" — which is often the regular classroom. General education teachers must also be able to generate ways to assist the student or make adaptations.

Following are some ideas to get started. As you read over the list, you will probably see ideas and techniques that you have used with other students in your classroom over the years; students who need modifications to assist them with their attention, learning, and behavior. These strategies will work with any student who may be experiencing trouble of one kind or another in your classroom. There is nothing magic about the list; the "magic" occurs when you find the idea or strategy that will help put the student's world back into perspective, which will make the days more manageable for everyone.

Fatigue

• *shorter day*
• *rest breaks*

Some children may not return to school on a full day schedule. If they choose to start by going half days, make sure that you get their best half day. If they are slow to get going in the morning, consider afternoon classes. If they opt to take only 1–2 classes, try to ensure that the classes are at a good time of the day and that they are classes that the student likes or was doing well in previously. This can help school reentry get off to a positive start. Whether the student attends for half or full days, make sure that short rest breaks are provided throughout the day and that a place, such as the nurse's station, is available for the student to lie down to rest as needed.

Memory/Organization

We all develop different ways to help us organize throughout the day so that we don't forget or neglect important things. Assisting a student with organizational strategies may be one of the most helpful things you can do for the student and for the family. Many of us use notebooks or calendars to jot down appointments and reminders; this is a good idea for students with memory and organizational difficulties as well. It is important, however, that the student not be solely responsible for this. Family members and school personnel may need to assist the student at the key points listed below.

When	What needs to be done	Who checks
before leaving home (a.m.)	go over list of what needs to be returned to school	parent
arrival at school	check what student needs to get started	teacher/case manager/aide
end of each class	write down assignments in notebook	teacher/ aide
before leaving school (p.m.)	check to see if student has assignments written down & that they have the appropriate books	teacher/ case manager/aide
arrival at home	help child get organized and started on homework assignments	parent

• extra books

Since it takes extra energy to carry books back and forth to school and extra effort to remember them, having an extra set of textbooks at home can be helpful. Important information in the texts can also be highlighted if they are purchased specifically for the student.

• backpack

A backpack is a useful article for carrying things to and from school, particularly for a student with motor problems. The backpack can be the identifiable article that the student keeps with him at all times.

• daily schedule

A schedule of the day's activities can be taped to the student's desk or inside the organization notebook to help remember the routine and any special activities.

• buddy system

A buddy system can be invaluable to a student with a brain injury. The "buddy" can be one or more students/peers with whom the teacher, the family and the student all feel comfortable. Use of a peer to prompt or remind the student is less obtrusive than constant adult intervention. Frequent intervention by adults usually means that less interaction with peers will occur, which can be detrimental to social skill development. Use of a buddy might also provide needed structure and assistance for the unexpected; fire drills, weather alerts and other emergency situations.

• limit changes

Reducing the number of changes in the student's routine will also be helpful. As previously mentioned, the "routine" is essential for a student with memory difficulties. Changes in routine may leave the student not knowing what to do or where to go.

Motor difficulties

• provide assistance with written tasks

Students who have residual problems with motor skills may find it difficult to complete written work in the classroom. Their motor problems may not allow them to work quickly or efficiently and the finished project may not be legible or reflect their effort. For some students, writing paper can be stabilized with masking tape or a piece of Dycem (nonskid material often used by occupational therapists). Students whose motor difficulties are more severe can benefit from using a computer or typewriter for writing and a calculator for math (see math section for more detailed information about the calculator).

• reduce written work

Even these assists may not be sufficient to help a student keep pace with the rest of the class. If this is the case, then other alternatives need to be explored. Consider reducing the written work that will be required. For example, writing spelling words in sentences is a typical classroom assignment. If the goal for the student is to learn how to spell 25 words, then the focus should be on spelling, not sentence construction. If a secondary goal is to improve sentence construction, then perhaps the student could practice writing/typing the words and use 5–10 of them in a sentence, rather than all 25. The end result is that the student: a) learns to spell the words; b) gets some practice with sentence construction; and c) keeps up with the rest of the class.

The same idea can be used in math. Rather than having a student copy and complete 30–50 math problems, 10–20 problems could be written out and picked by the teacher to represent new skills being learned. If the student can demonstrate mastery with those 10–20 problems, is it necessary to do 50? Class time and effort will be spent learning additional skills and evening time can then be spent with the family, rather than on homework assignments.

• the buddy system

The buddy system also works well when adapting for motor difficulties, as the "buddy" can become a peer secretary, who writes down dictated responses. This works extremely well for the student who would otherwise take enormous amounts of time to complete written work, even when using a computer keyboard or calculator.

• dictation

Student helpers who volunteer to be a peer secretary must be instructed to write down exactly what the student dictates, regardless of whether it is correct. In this way, the teacher will have an accurate picture of the student's abilities and can identify which areas continue to need work. If a teacher assistant or volunteer is working in the classroom, these individuals can take dictation from the student who, otherwise, might fall behind in written work because of motor problems. Compensation for motor problems can also be accomplished by allowing the student to complete some work orally.

• extra time

Sometimes a student's motor problems are mild and do not require any specific adaptations, but do require that extra time be given to complete assignments. Arranging study halls after a class that consistently requires written work (Literature, English, Math) might be beneficial; or providing assistance from a teacher aide, peer or resource teacher near the end of the school day may also be helpful.

If a student works more slowly than the average student, try to avoid timed tests and other activities. They will not provide an accurate picture of the student's abilities and knowledge. (See note-taking in next section.)

Reading

• books on tape

If a student had learning problems prior to the injury, it is possible that the problems will be more pronounced afterward. In reading, inefficient word decoding skills and/or a slower reading rate will contribute to a student's inability to comprehend the material and keep pace with the rest of the class. Books on tape are readily available for text books and leisure reading materials through many state associations for persons with visual impairments. In addition, many of these organizations can provide taped materials for persons with physical impairments and reading disabilities. The student with reading problems can follow along in the text while listening to the tape on a set of headphones, while other students in the class are reading the material. Leisure reading material on tape will encourage the student to listen to the same books that peers may be reading, which will contribute to an increase in general knowledge and age appropriate information. Discussion of the book with peers may also assist the student in social interactions.

• adapt tests

Students with reading difficulties will also need to have adaptations made when they are required to take (read) tests. The test can be administered orally by a teacher aide or adult volunteer and the student allowed to provide oral answers, since writing skills are usually weaker than reading skills.

• help with note taking

A student with weak reading/writing skills will need assistance in classes which require note taking. Important text information can be highlighted in the student's personal text books; probably the most helpful assist, however, is a carbon or Xerox copy of another student's notes. The process should be discussed ahead of time with both students and their parents, so that everyone understands and agrees on the process. Documentation of this and other adaptations in the student's educational plan is a good idea, particularly for future teachers. Although the student may need help with the actual reading of the notes, they will serve as a study guide and a summary for the student and others working with him prior to taking a test.

• extra instruction

A student with a reading disability can often benefit from remedial reading instruction. Memory problems can interfere, however, with the ability to utilize typical approaches to reading that incorporate the use of phonics, blending sounds and the memorization of sight words. If this is the case, the instructor might try to teach reading by "chunking information" or using word families such as fight, right, sight, light, etc.

Math

Students with reading disabilities or memory problems will often have difficulty with the memorization of basic math facts. Certainly, a teacher will want to continue working on these with the student, but not to the point where the child falls hopelessly behind the rest of the class. Whether a student counts on fingers, uses a math fact sheet, practices with flashcards or uses a calculator, the end result is the same; the student arrives at the correct answer and tries to commit it to memory. Once a student is sure of the answer, time will not be spent using the calculator or counting fingers; the student will simply write it down. On the other hand, if the student is unable to commit these facts to memory, you have provided an appropriate alternative to use when there is no one around to help.

• try using a calculator

This becomes especially important as students reach adolescence and need a reliable alternative for dealing with math in activities of daily living (going to the movie, the store, or out for pizza with friends). In this day and age, no one thinks twice about someone using a calculator — at any age. If, after several years of instruction, a student is still experiencing problems with math facts, it would be a wiser use of teacher and student time to place more emphasis on teaching functional calculator skills. Primarily, this involves the use of story problems (written or oral) so that the student learns how and when to use certain operations, particularly for math in activities of daily living.

One final word about math and calculators — the calculator is also useful and sometimes necessary for a student with a physical impairment. Even though a student may show good potential for memorizing math facts, if the physical impairment is severe enough to significantly affect a student's work rate and written work is difficult to read, then use of a calculator may be more appropriate. Ask yourself, "How will this student function most appropriately, efficiently and accurately when dealing with math as an adult?" If motor skills will interfere with the student's math performance, shouldn't we be providing instruction that will allow an individual to function in "the least restrictive" but most productive and satisfying way as an adult?

Social Skills

- *organizing a buddy system*

Use of the buddy system for redeveloping appropriate social skills can be helpful, particularly in unstructured situations (playground, hallway, lunchroom) where the student may be prone to having difficulty. Again, continual intervention by an adult may draw unwanted attention to the student and can discourage peers from interacting. A "buddy" can redirect, prompt and cue less obtrusively than an adult. When using the buddy system, it may be helpful/necessary to utilize several students so that no one student feels overly responsible; it will also be important to choose students who genuinely care about their classmate and are interested in working through the difficulties. As always, it is a good idea to notify the parents of all students involved so that they have knowledge and understanding of these activities. Also, since we know that unstructured activities tend to create problems for many students with brain injuries, it would be wise for school personnel to increase supervision in these areas, at least initially, to ensure the safety of the student and to intervene if necessary.

When trying to develop or improve social relationships and interactions, try to use real life situations rather than setting up something artificial, so that learning will be more meaningful to the student. For example, sitting with a small group of students at lunch (which many of us tend to use as a social time) may provide insight as to where problems might occur. There are certainly other students within the classroom or school who could also benefit from social skills feedback in a group like this. A "buddy" or case manager may be able to provide helpful suggestions to the student during lunch or immediately following. Special clubs or groups may also provide opportunities to interact; teachers involved need to communicate with each other in order to identify areas which need work and to identify areas that are improving.

A case manager or social worker for the student can help coordinate efforts and communication between the family, school and medical personnel. The case manager can also serve as a "counselor" for the student when necessary. There may be times when the student feels overwhelmed, frustrated, embarrassed or angry and needs a safe place to go and a trusted person with whom to talk. The case manager can also keep other professionals apprised of the student's feelings and specific areas of difficulty.

Attention

- *shorten assignments*

A student's ability to pay attention, especially for extended periods of time, may be impaired after a brain injury. Providing shorter assignments, or breaking assignments down into smaller tasks may assist the student in maintaining better attention. Many adults find that they are better able to attend to material if they are given short breaks between sessions — remember the last all-day conference that you attended? Some students find it motivating to work with a timer, i.e., "see how much of this you can finish before the timer rings... you will receive extra points...or I will give you a break...or you will receive a sticker...or you can listen to music on your

Walkman for five minutes or..." The ideas can vary — use your imagination and knowledge about what motivates the student.

- **minimize distractions**

All of us experience distractions that cause problems with attention as we work; noises, conversations, activity in the room or out the window. Providing a quiet corner of the room or a study carrel may help reduce these distractions. Some individuals (including the one writing this chapter) are better able to focus if there is "white noise" or soft music in the background. This can be accomplished easily in the classroom by providing the student with a tape and a set of headphones.

Behavior

Parents and teachers frequently identify behavior problems as one of their major concerns after a brain injury occurs. This is not surprising as we begin to recognize and acknowledge the frustrating and bewildering incidents that occur daily for a person who has sustained a brain injury. You may be dealing with a student who does not perceive or understand the changes in their performance or, perhaps, a student who is painfully aware of the abilities and skills that have been lost. At any rate, there are some things to keep in mind in order to avoid or minimize the problems that occur.

- **avoid changes in routine**

Avoid changes in routine whenever possible. Remember that routine and structure are critical for someone who has memory problems. Changes in the routine may increase the student's confusion and disorganization. On the other hand, we live in a world where change is constant and things are not always predictable, so when a change in routine is necessary, provide as much transition time as possible to help the student get ready mentally. Offer additional help and structure for the change and enlist the student's help if possible, i.e., "We are going next door for a movie instead of going outside because the weather is bad. Will you help me by taking the videotape over to Ms. Smith's room?" Or, whenever possible, remind the student, "In five minutes, we will be leaving for science class."

• give choices

It also helps to give the student choices whenever possible to increase a sense of control over life and activities, i.e. , "We won't be able to go outside today because the weather is bad — would you like to watch a video with Ms. Smith's class, listen to your Walkman or use the computer in our classroom?"

Giving choices can also be helpful in terms of completing assignments, i.e., "You need to finish your spelling words or complete the math problems in your workbook. Which would you like to tackle first?" Giving choices and providing transitions will help you avoid getting into power struggles with the student.

• be flexible in expectations

Don't be afraid to change or reduce your expectations for a student if they seem unrealistic or if the student is consistently unsuccessful. It doesn't mean that you've "given in" or lost the battle — only that you've made an attempt to help the student experience success. All of us will find numerous ways to avoid work that is too difficult and no one wants to experience repeated failure. We all want to be successful at our work; school *is* the student's work.

Behavior problems can also occur when the student becomes fatigued and feels ill-equipped to deal with an assignment or activity. Try to assign difficult classes earlier in the day or at a time when the student is at his/her best. Initiating, problem solving and attending will all be easier if the student is rested and alert.

• diary for student

Use of a diary may provide the student with an additional outlet. It gives the student a place to record feelings, thoughts and reactions and it may provide some insight for parents and professionals. These thoughts and feelings can be discussed later with a specific teacher, case manager, counselor, or parent so that the student receives some feedback and closure. The diary might also be used to describe incidents that occur during the day (bad ones and good ones) so that these can be used as examples to the student in shaping future behavior, i.e., "What could you have done/said differently to avoid this conflict?" or "What do you think it was that you said/did that helped this situation?" Remember, if you decide to use a diary, the student may need help recording and organizing thoughts and ideas.

In general, when dealing with any student in class, it is important to focus on the concept or skill that you want the student to learn and find the most efficient, effective (and fun!) route to the mastery of that concept. This will help increase success, save time and energy, and avoid frustration for both student and teacher.

Working with the Neuropsychologist

by Gary F. Wolcott, M.Ed. & Marilyn Lash, M.S.W.

What is a neuropsychologist?

A neuropsychologist is a psychologist who specializes in defining the *relationships* between a person's brain and his/her functioning (behavior) in the world. The neuropsychologist can evaluate how the brain injury affects the student's ability to:

- learn
- communicate
- plan and organize
- relate to others

The neuropsychologist uses a variety of tests (games, puzzles, responses to words and images) to understand how the brain injury affects the student's ability to function.

To be a neuropsychologist one must earn a Ph.D. in psychology and complete specialized training and internships in neuropsychology.

The neuropsychologist is different than a *neurologist* who is a physician that focuses on the physical structure of the brain and nervous system.

The neuropsychologist is different than a *psychologist* who has the same basic training, but has not specialized in neuropsychology. A psychologist may not be able to do the more detailed evaluations needed for a student with a brain injury.

It is important to note that I.Q. and achievement tests (often given by general psychologists) are not always helpful in evaluating a student with a brain injury because significant parts measure what the child has learned in the past. **Often a student who has had a brain injury *does not lose* the academic knowledge gained prior to injury. Thus, the test scores on the sections of the I.Q. tests which rely on previously learned material (such as vocabulary, general information, social comprehension) may show little or no loss. This can give a misleading picture of the student's ability to function in the classroom and to learn new information.**

When to ask for a neuropsychological evaluation

- When a child has acquired a moderate to severe brain injury
- When a child has sustained a mild traumatic brain injury and is having trouble with attention, learning, behavior or emotions.
- Any time significant problems or changes in functioning arise that the team of educators and parents cannot explain or work with effectively.

When you hear comments by the:

Parent	"He's failing and I don't understand why!"
Teacher	"I've tried everything in class and nothing seems to work!"
Team	"He does well in some situations but terrible in others!"

then it is important to involve a neuropsychologist to help define the problem and develop strategies to help the student.

Helpful tips

- If the child is still in a hospital or rehabilitation center, ask that a neuropsychological evaluation be done before the child is discharged.
- If the child is home or has returned to school (and received treatment from a rehabilitation center), ask for a copy of any neuropsychological evaluation reports.

How to select a neuropsychologist

- The school district may have an ongoing contract with a neuropsychologist. If this is the case, then the selection process is already complete.

- If a neuropsychologist has not been identified, then the educational team and the parents may want to contact the state's professional psychology association, the local chapter of the head injury foundation, or talk with other educators in your area.

- Ask if the neuropsychologist:
  - is experienced with school age students with acquired brain injuries?
  - is familiar with the special education system?
  - is willing to focus the evaluation process on the practical issues of the student's classroom performance, social relationships, and behavior?

What to share with the neuropsychologist

1) A completed Worksheet: *Transition Back to School Following Brain Injury. (See worksheet section of this book.)*

2) A description of current school programs and activities and a detailed educational history.

3) Current records of grades and any other information about the student's present classroom performance.

4) The student's individualized educational plan and quarterly reports if the student is receiving special education services.

5) Written descriptions from educators' observations of the student, including when and where problems occur.

6) A list of concerns or questions about the student and his/her strengths and needs.

What to ask the neuropsychologist

- Is there a brain injury?

- How does the brain injury affect the student's:
  - work in groups
  - need for individualized instruction
  - ability to learn new materials
  - efforts in timed tests/quizzes
  - control over behavior
  - ability to participate in group situations
  - social interactions with friends
  - ability to complete assignments on time
  - stamina during school day
  - impact on performance and side effects of medications
  - emotional adjustment and sense of well-being

- How can teachers work effectively with the student?
  - describe the student's current strengths and needs
  - explain the student's most effective learning styles
  - give examples of what teachers can do in the classroom that will emphasize the student's strengths
  - suggest activities where peers can help
  - provide suggestions for parents/family members at home

- What will be the most effective way for the neuropsychologist to conduct the evaluation?
  - visit the school and observe the student
  - receive a video tape of the student in school or at home in a challenging situation
  - conduct testing in a number of shorter sessions rather than one long session

What should you get from the neuropsychologist?

- Specific suggestions and techniques for
  - classroom strategies to assist student in completing assignments
  - methods to improve new learning
  - effective ways to prompt/redirect student
  - management of inappropriate or difficult behavior
  - guidelines for learning in various settings
    - one-to-one
    - small group
  - use of adaptive devices for memory, communication, organization
  - alternative methods of student evaluation
    - open book tests
    - untimed tests
    - oral vs. written
    - pictures vs. words
    - multiple choice vs. essay
    - techniques for reading: silent vs. auditory

Who pays for the neuropsychological evaluation?

This is a difficult issue. Please consider the following ideas.

- Get the initial neuropsychological evaluation done while the child is still in the hospital or rehabilitation center. Health insurance is more likely to pay for testing done in a medical setting.

How often should it be done?

- If an evaluation is done, it creates baseline information which is invaluable in reassessment and educational planning later.

- Keep in mind that a student will be changing and most likely, improving as time goes on. Therefore, follow-up neuropsychological evaluations may be more effective in assisting with the actual planning after the child returns to school.

- Arrange to have the neuropsychological evaluation done on an outpatient basis if the family has medical insurance and it covers such services (even if it pays for only part and school pays for co-insurance portion).

- The information from a neuropsychological evaluation can actually save the school district money by providing critical information for building *effective and efficient* educational plans that directly meet the student's needs.

Helping Parents and Family Members

by Marilyn Lash, M.S.W.

As children enter or return to school following a traumatic brain injury, parents expect that the worst is behind them. Few parents forget the horror of seeing their child injured and the fear that their child will not survive. Even years later, parents can still describe in painful detail their feelings of anguish and helplessness during the agonizing wait for news at the hospital. Seeing their child lying unresponsive and comatose is a living nightmare for parents that is only worsened by guilt over failure to protect their child from harm.

Many parents spend long days and nights at the hospital while their other children manage as best they can at home, often in the substitute care of relatives or neighbors. More seriously injured children are often transferred from local hospitals to trauma centers in urban areas for specialized care. This creates even more upheaval in the family's life. Living in motel rooms, sleeping in hospital waiting rooms, and taking turns at their child's bedside are physically and emotionally exhausting. Many parents hang on simply by holding on to the hope that if they can only get their child home, then everything will be all right.

A survey by the Research and Training Center in Rehabilitation and Childhood Trauma in 1992 was completed by 68 parents whose children had been injured seriously enough to be hospitalized in a pediatric trauma center or to be admitted to an inpatient rehabilitation program. It found that families needed more information about the injury and its effects on their child. The top four needs for information cited were: 1) the meaning of their child's diagnosis; 2) information about community organizations and resources;

Families are not prepared for what to expect after a brain injury. Survival is not the same as recovery. Changes can be major or subtle, but their child is somehow different now.

3) availability of state and federal programs for children with disabilities; and 4) expectations for their child's future.

These needs underscore how unprepared families are for the physical, emotional, cognitive, and behavioral changes that may result from a brain injury. The grieving process that families experience is incomplete because the child survives but is changed. The process is further complicated by the many questions concerning prognosis that physicians and other health care professionals are unable to answer. Little research has been done to study the long-term outcomes of children after brain injuries.

This uncertainty creates many conflicts and anxieties for families. The tendency of many children to make remarkable physical progress often masks more subtle changes in the child's ability to process information, organize tasks, control impulses and monitor behaviors. For children whose brain injuries are considered less severe, and particularly those who did not have the dramatic stage of coma, subtle changes in emotions, behaviors and learning may puzzle families and educators. These difficulties usually become more apparent as the child enters or returns to school and is increasingly challenged to learn new information, adjust to multiple settings, interact with many students and teachers, and is expected to meet academic standards.

School is a critical environment for the child and family. It is the setting where children learn to function outside the shelter and protection of their homes and develop the social skills necessary for interpersonal relationships among peers. It is the arena where students gradually develop the skills and self-reliance that will enable them to become independent in preparation for adulthood. School also is the arena where the long-term and latent cognitive effects of a child's brain injury are most likely to become evident as the challenge of learning becomes increasingly complex.

The child who has had a brain injury is particularly at risk for lowered academic performance and social isolation which can then result in lowered self-esteem. Depression is a common reaction among students with traumatic brain injuries who are aware of

"I saw the teacher as the key and link to my child's future."

their inability to achieve pre-injury levels of academic performance and social integration.

Educators are critical resources for interventions, guidance and support for students with traumatic brain injuries and for their parents and siblings. Educators can be the pivotal influence to prepare peers, develop support systems, identify needed interventions, design compensatory strategies, and develop academic and functional goals. It is important for educators to collaborate closely with parents or guardians throughout this process, yet too often the process of educational planning and negotiation for special education and related services becomes an adversarial one or occurs only after the student has had major difficulties or failures. The following section discusses primary concerns that have been identified by families for their child's return to school following a brain injury and during subsequent transitions in school between teachers, grades and schools.

Blame and guilt among families

Traumatic brain injuries among children most frequently result from motor vehicle related collisions. Children are injured by motor vehicles while riding as occupants, when struck as pedestrians or as bicyclists. These mechanisms involve speed and impact. Falls from heights can also result in brain injuries among children. Common causes are falls down flights of stairs, out of windows, and off balconies.

Injuries are not isolated events. Not only may the child's brain be injured, but other body regions may be damaged as well. However, unlike bone fractures, cuts, bruises, and even internal injuries, brain injuries cause irreparable damage. The physical damage to a child is compounded by the emotional aftermath. Other persons — parents, siblings or peers — may be injured and hospitalized as well. Just at the time when a young child may most need the comfort and presence of a parent, they may be unavailable and separated. The death of a parent, sibling or peer can be devastating to the child who survives. The hospitalized child is even isolated from the mourning rituals of funerals. The full impact may not be felt

"I still think, 'If only I had...' It's been three years and I still have nightmares about the crash."

until the child leaves the protective environment of the hospital and experiences the loss at home, in school and in the community.

The tragedy of these injuries is that they can be prevented. Children wearing safety belts, placed in child safety seats, and wearing bicycle helmets are less likely to be seriously injured. Safety measures such as protective rails and guards can protect children from falls. Parents experience terrible anguish and guilt over their failure to protect their child from harm as they relive "if only I had" scenarios.

A child's injury affects every member of the family in some way. The grieving and adjustment process for families is described in the guide *When your child is seriously injured....the emotional impact on families.* (See Resource section of this book.) Based on the input and experiences of families, it traces the reactions of families from arrival at the emergency room through the child's hospitalization and planning for discharge. It is recommended to give educators insight into the emotional trauma that families experience, including siblings, and contains many practical suggestions for coping.

The process of a family's grieving is unpredictable. Marital stress is common when spouses cope in different ways. Some parents recall feeling so totally overwhelmed that they isolated themselves at home, cried constantly and avoided friends and neighbors. Others coped by becoming "super busy". As friends or teachers admired how well they were doing, they were terrified of falling apart if they stopped. In their grief, families may seek someone to blame, to become the target of their anger. It is possible for schools or teachers to become this target just as a physician or nurse was at the hospital. It is important to understand that the anger may stem from a deeper grief and rage about what has happened to the child.

Denial is a term used to describe the feeling that, "It can't be true, it's not real, it can't be as bad as they say." Professionals in health care and educators often view denial as a negative symptom and become frustrated with parents because they "aren't facing the facts." Denial is actually a protective stage that can help families function as they gather the emotional strength to deal with their losses.

The word "acceptance" is often used, but is a difficult and lengthy process. How long it takes to reach this stage is different for each parent. One way of describing it is the point at which parents have a realistic understanding of their child's abilities and limitations. It is that period when the injured child's condition and care are no longer the central focus in a family's life. While the child may always have special needs, they do not necessarily take priority over the needs of others in the family, but are balanced within the needs of all for care, attention, support and love.

How does rehabilitation differ for children?

Rehabilitation is a long-term process that will continue throughout the child's development and has no defined end point. Discharge from an acute hospital or rehabilitation program does not signal a child's recovery from a traumatic brain injury. Rather, discharge from the hospital marks the beginning of the next stage of rehabilitation that will occur in the child's home and at school.

Rehabilitation services are very different for children than for adults. There are not many pediatric rehabilitation programs specializing in traumatic brain injury. According to the National Pediatric Trauma Registry, more children with four or more functional limitations are discharged directly home from trauma centers than are transferred to in-patient rehabilitation programs. The leading diagnosis among these children is head injury.

Many families are able to provide physical care at home despite the child's difficulties in mobility, dressing, bathing, speech, vision, hearing, cognition or behavior. Children are lighter and smaller; this enables families to provide care at home that would otherwise be impossible for adults. Rehabilitation services may be arranged on an out-patient basis. Still another factor is the limits of health insurance benefits for children. Many policies do not cover in-patient rehabilitation services for children; thus, limiting options for families.

Consequently, educators will encounter children with brain injuries who have spent many weeks or months in rehabilitation hospitals and programs before returning home. However, they will also meet children who return directly home from the acute care hospital or trauma center. *Length of stay in a hospital does not determine whether a child will need special education after a traumatic brain injury.* In fact, the family whose child has returned directly home after a short hospital stay may be even *less* prepared to assess the long-term consequences of their child's injury and be *less* prepared to discuss educational needs with the school.

Families lack prior experience with special education

The vast majority of children who have traumatic brain injuries have no preexisting conditions. Consequently, their parents are inexperienced with the "special needs" system and may consider it a program primarily for children with birth disorders or mental retardation.

The primary question that families ask is, "How will my child's brain injury affect his/her ability to learn?" Unfortunately, medical and rehabilitation experts can not give parents precise or definitive information. Although P.L. 101-476, the Individuals with Disabilities Education Act, specifically creates a special classification for children with traumatic brain injuries, the provision of services still needs to be negotiated individually with the child's local school and educational system. Families need basic information about:

- What is special education?
- How do I apply for my child?
- What supports and services do my child need?
- What is an individualized education plan?
- How can I tell if my child is learning?
- How can I measure my child's progress?
- Who pays for this?

Family's concerns about qualifications of educators

"I was really nervous about Sara going to school. I had stayed with her every night at the hospital. Then I left my job to care for her at home. School was the first place where I couldn't stay with her. I was afraid to let her be on her own, but I knew I had to. I was probably more nervous than she was. She wanted to be with her friends and see her teachers again. It's hard for me to let go after we almost lost her."

Families often refer to discharge from the hospital or rehabilitation program as the second "crisis of injury" because the responsibility for the child's ongoing care and continuing needs shifts to them. During the medical crisis, families draw reassurance from the multiple specialists caring for their child. Knowing that their child is "in the hands of experts" brings some comfort. By contrast, when the child returns to school, families typically find that educators and school staff have little or no prior experience or training in traumatic brain injury. This creates considerable anxiety and even alarm. "How will the school know what my child needs?"

Unfortunately, this contrast is often reinforced by recommendations from medical and rehabilitation experts that specialized services and programs in traumatic brain injury are needed for the child at school. Recommendations may be made for a specialized classroom, expensive testing, and special programming that are unavailable at the local school. Families are ill prepared to judge whether alternative methods of instruction and services proposed by the school are adequate.

The time required by schools to gather medical information, complete educational testing, process applications for services, and construct educational plans often takes much longer than families expect. It contrasts with the rapid pace of the child's earlier medical treatment. Meanwhile, many parents become anxious about the effects of these delays upon their child's progress and recovery.

Educators can build confidence in parents by showing an interest and willingness to learn about the effects of traumatic brain injuries. Parents stress that it is the interest, flexibility and commitment by teachers that foster positive relationships. While parents may prefer that teachers already have specialized skills and training in brain injuries, many recognize the limitations of schools and teachers' experiences. When teachers are receptive to suggestions for reading, obtain information from state head injury chapters, make themselves available for consultation with rehabilitation staff, inquire about strategies used by parents, and ask insightful questions, then many parents are reassured and feel that their child is less "at risk" in school.

Timing of child's return to school

Each brain injury is different. Any child whose behaviors and performance at school change following a blow to the head needs to be evaluated for a traumatic brain injury.

The length of a child's hospitalization is not a predictor of what the child will need upon returning to school. The severity of the initial injury is not the same as the severity of the resulting disability. Some very seriously injured children recover quite well. Others with less severe brain injuries have long lasting difficulties. The length of time that a child is absent following an injury, however, can affect how educators and families perceive the child's needs. When a child is in critical condition, particularly when a coma extends for weeks or months, schools are alerted to the possibility that this child may have a serious disability. The child who is seen briefly in the emergency room and sent home, or admitted overnight for observation after a blow to the head is more readily assumed to be "all right." This is not always true.

The transfer of information between medical specialists and educators frequently is problematic. School staff often assume that the medical staff will advise them of what is needed, while medical staff wait for the school to contact them. Too often, the result is poor communication and planning between hospitals and schools. When schools do receive medical reports, they are frequently written in such technical medical jargon that they are of little use for educational planning.

Medical and educational institutions are completely different entities in terms of how they are staffed, financed and operated. These fundamental differences can lead to conflicts in expectations and goals as the injured child moves from one setting to the other.

As a last resort, families often become the link for information between hospital staff, follow-up appointments and school staff. However, families may not know what information is needed, how to collect it, and what to do with it. A detailed outline of the physical, sensory, communicative, cognitive and behavioral effects of brain injuries was developed for families in the guide, *When your child goes to school after an injury.* (See Resource section of this book.) It lists questions for families to ask educators about their child's abilities and performance at school. Educators may wish to use this as a guide.

Miracle of survival

Families frequently describe their child's survival and recovery from a life threatening injury as miraculous. Having seen their child close to death — in a coma — breathing only with the help of a respirator — wired to machines and hooked into tubes — is a terrifying experience. Even when their child slowly emerged from coma, many families were given cautious predictions about functional abilities for mobility, speech, communication and self-care. Having watched a child beat the grim odds given by medical experts, it is not surprising that many parents expect the same miraculous recovery to extend into school.

This "need to hope" is also a reflection of how weary and exhausted families can be by the time a child is ready to return to school. Going to school may signal a respite for families from the child's daily care and supervision, and from the stress of lowered finances due to time off from work and unpaid medical bills. Consequently, many families are unprepared to face the difficulties that their child may experience in school. If the school adopts an attitude of, "Let's wait and see" how the child does in school, the family may be only too willing to "hope for the best." However, this delay can result in lost opportunities for early intervention for educational planning and the student may be quickly discouraged by early failures and difficulty adjusting to the demands of the classroom and curriculum.

Families need careful and supportive guidance by school staff to make sure that the child's needs are thoroughly assessed and that educational plans are designed as soon as possible to address the child's special learning needs. The initial "honeymoon period" between schools and families often bursts when it becomes evident that the child is having serious difficulties. Too often, negotiations deteriorate into legal battles between schools and families. The following suggestions are designed to prevent this from occurring and to encourage a partnership for educational planning between parents and educators.

Action Steps
You Can Take

Listen to families

Parents know their child best. They not only have the pre-injury comparison of their child, but they have seen their child's reactions and progress through the various stages of treatment and recovery. Parents may detect subtle changes before they are apparent to others. This is particularly important with younger children who are unable to express their needs clearly. Families also have opportunities to observe their child's cognitive process in many different settings and circumstances. They see how their child functions during days and evenings, when tired or alert, in concentrated silence or with distracting interruptions. Parents and family members have experience in developing cueing systems, designing strategies to aid memory, and helping children finish tasks. Parents' observations may yield information that is far more practical than testing and achievement scores that represent the child's capacity in a structured and controlled setting for specific functions.

Carryover and consistency between families and educators is essential for the child who has had a brain injury. Therefore, it is important for educators and families to share their methods so that the family can reinforce effective techniques used in the classroom. Similarly, educators may find home based strategies that parents have found effective to be applicable with modifications to the classroom setting.

Help the parents/family set up a record keeping system

Many children return for follow-up visits to medical specialists long after their injuries yet reports are frequently not shared with schools. The family is the critical link and can facilitate communication by requesting copies of reports and delivering them directly. A child's recovery is likely to extend over years. Families will meet with many specialists, educators, and consultants. Children will have many assessments done, testing performed, reports written and recommendations made. None of this information is likely to be stored in one place and can be just about impossible to track down years later. As students progress through grades and various schools, bits and pieces inevitably get lost or separated. Parents and family members will be the only constant source of historical information over the years that can influence the student's access to services and support.

Families and educators can benefit right in the beginning by setting up an educational record in a flexible three ring binder that remains the property of the parent. This record will grow as the child moves from teacher to teacher, grade to grade and school to school. Educators and families can strategize what information is most useful to record. This can provide a critical and comprehensive record that can be used by families and educators to track a child's progress, compare interventions and outcomes, and record important dates, names and addresses. It provides a continuous record that will help identify patterns, spot potential problems and compare programs and results.

Suggestions for sections to include are:

- description of pre-injury abilities and performance in school and at home
- description of medical care and rehabilitation
- description of current medications
- community resources
- state and federal programs
- description of current strengths and needs
- past and current academic grades and performance
- special education directors, teachers, teacher aids, and tutors
- special education services recommended and received
- related services such as transportation, therapies, counseling, etc.

Provide support as students, parents and family members alter their hopes and dreams

"I just don't know what's possible now — how it will affect her future. It's hard to give up the hopes that we have built over the years."

Uncertainty about the future is one of the most difficult aspects of brain injury for families. The loss of hopes and dreams is painful. The age when the child is injured is a factor. Parents of children who were injured when very young speak of lost potential. When preschool age children are injured, or even very young elementary school children, much is still unknown about the child's skills, abilities and interests. The child's personality is still emerging as communication skills develop, habits form, and unique character traits appear. Parents speak wistfully of not knowing how their child "might have been" had the injury not occurred.

A particular sadness expressed by parents of children injured during their earlier formative years is the sadness of watching younger siblings surpass them in motor skills, communication and speech, and cognitive abilities. Siblings of children injured at a young age also quickly lose their recall of the child prior to injury. The competition that parents expect and tolerate between siblings has a bittersweet edge after an injury when the younger siblings' abilities surpass the older child who has been injured.

Aspirations for jobs, interests in vocational training and careers, and hopes for college already may be defined, especially for adolescents. A brain injury may seriously threaten these plans and force families, students and educators to reevaluate whether they are realistic. Peer pressure among adolescents can make it especially difficult for the student who has had a brain injury to fit in and keep up with classmates. Appearance, dating, and sexuality become primary concerns among adolescents and the injured student may no longer be as attractive to and accepted by peers.

Too many high school students who were injured close to graduation accept high school diplomas without realizing that this disqualifies them for additional special educational services. This premature graduation can readily backfire as students find that vocational rehabilitation services in the community are not as readily available as special education in public schools. Any family with an adolescent approaching graduation age needs careful advice and guidance from educators and advocates on whether acceptance of a diploma affects eligibility for further educational services and vocational options. A transition plan that identifies how the student will acquire the necessary skills for adulthood is needed.

Explore the special issues among foster families by asking about the student's history and supports provided by social service agencies

Child abuse is a primary cause of brain injury among infants and preschool children. Foster and adoptive families typically lack complete medical records and family histories for these children. Many abused children have multiple disabilities including damaged vision or hearing as well as motor difficulties. Multiple foster homes and temporary placements can contribute to behavioral problems and exacerbate emotional disturbances among abused children. This can contribute to delinquent patterns and even expulsion from school. The significance of early brain injuries caused by beatings or batterings may be overlooked as the child ages. Because children's brains are especially vulnerable to injury if shaken, abused or beaten at an early age, it is important for foster families and educators to question the relationship between early physical abuse and later learning and behavioral difficulties.

Remember siblings and encourage parents to evaluate their needs

Brothers and sisters are often the forgotten victims of injuries. With the primary concern and attention directed at the injured child, siblings easily can be overlooked. The turmoil at home inevitably affects siblings. Young siblings mistakenly may believe that they are responsible for the injury since young children's magical thinking often confuses cause and effect. Siblings may have witnessed the injury and have recurrent nightmares, fears, or trouble sleeping. Siblings may be jealous of the attention focused on the injured child and angry at disruptions in the family's routine. Older siblings may have additional responsibilities of caring for others and managing the household while parents are at the hospital.

These stresses may become evident at school as the grades of siblings drop, as attention wanders, or as behaviors change. Families may fail to inform the teachers of siblings about the family crisis. Consequently, it is important to inform the teachers of siblings when schools are advised of a child's injury. School staff can then be alert to changes in siblings' behavior and grades and provide additional attention, support, and counseling.

Summary

Families and educators share the goal of helping the student learn, develop skills, and explore his/her potential. This can best be done as partners in planning, educating, and evaluating the student's needs, abilities and difficulties. When a student has special educational needs as a result of a brain injury this partnership between families and educators becomes even more important. Each has an expertise and viewpoint that can help guide the student, develop effective plans, and bring insight to help work through difficulties and find needed resources. After all, both parent and educators share the ultimate goal of preparing the student for adulthood.

Transition Planning Worksheet:

Transition Back to School Following a Brain Injury

by Gary F. Wolcott, M.Ed.

and Sue Pearson, M.A.

This worksheet is designed to help the educational team plan for the student's return to school. The information needed to complete this worksheet may come from many sources including family members, medical and rehabilitation staff, other educators who have worked with the student in the past, and by direct observation and discussion with the student. Brain injuries can cause impairments in all areas of the student's cognitive, social/behavioral, and sensorimotor functioning with unique and sometimes unanticipated consequences. Only a holistic look at the student's history, medical/rehabilitative services, and current strengths/needs can reveal the specific pattern of disabilities confronting the student with a brain injury.

Date:
Student Name:
Age/Grade Now: *Age/Grade at Time of Injury:*

1. Description of Circumstances Surrounding Injury

The events and experiences of a child's injury often have long term emotional consequences that the teacher and guidance counselor should be aware of when working with the student and her/his family.

Date of injury:

_____

Describe all physical injuries:

_____

_____

Describe events leading to student's injury:

_____

_____

_____

_____

In this description, please consider:

- *Involvement of family members/close friends?*
- *Was someone found to be at fault? Have formal charges been brought? Is there current litigation?*
- *Were others injured? Did anyone die?*
- *Was alcohol/drug use a factor?*

2. Description of Family

A brain injury to a student is a traumatic event in the life of a family. The injury, hospitalization/rehabilitation process, and the student's resulting disabilities have a social and emotional impact on each family member. It is an event that often consumes the time, financial, and emotional resources of the entire family.

Who lives at home?	*Age*	*Last Grade Completed*	*Occupation*
Mother			
Father			
Siblings (age, grade in school)			
Others (relationship to student)			

Is the family coping with other long term medical or care issues? Describe:

_____

_____

Describe the family's strengths which can be built upon to establish a school-family partnership:

_____

_____

_____

_____

3. Time Frames

The severity of a brain injury does not necessarily equal the student's ultimate level of disability. Some students with very severe injuries recover completely while others with a mild traumatic injury may have severe disabilities. However, most go through a lengthy recovery period which is affected by the severity of injuries.

Define Time frames	Days/Months	Dates From/To
Length of Coma		
Time in Acute Hospital		
Time in Rehabilitation Program		
Recovery Time at Home/Outpatient Services		

4. Description of Medical Care & Rehabilitation

Define Services/Contacts/Records	*Name/Phone of Contact*	Records Rec'd
Acute Hospital		
Physical Therapy		☐
Speech/Language Therapy		☐
Occupational Therapy		☐
Neuropsychological/Psychological Services		☐
Counseling for adjustment to disabiliites		☐
Other		☐
Rehabilitation Program		
Physical Therapy		☐
Speech/Language Therapy		☐
Occupational Therapy		☐
Neuropsychological/Psychological Services		☐
Educational & Vocational		☐
Counseling for adjustment to disabiliites		☐
Other		☐
Outpatient Services		
Physical Therapy		☐
Speech/Language Therapy		☐
Occupational Therapy		☐
Neuropsychological Services		☐
Vocational		☐
Other		☐

4. Description of Medical Care & Rehabilitation *(continued)*

Define Current Medical Status   *Description of Services/Treatment*

Medical/Nursing

Medications

Seizure Activity

Assistive Devices

Behavioral Status

Other

5. Description of *Pre-injury* Functioning

Define Developmental History   *Age*

Early Childhood Development

Disabilities Prior to Injury

Prior Significant Illness/Injury

Change in Right or Left Handedness

Define School History Prior to Injury

Achievement Test Scores   *Dates Administered:*

reading   *Grade level performance:*

math   *Grade level performance:*

written work   *Grade level performance:*

other   *Grade level performance:*

History of Special Education Services   *Date of Last Education Plan (IEP):*

Name/Phone – Chair of Committee   *Name/Phone – Last Teacher(s)*

5. Description of *Pre-injury* Functioning *(continued)*

Define Social/Family Functioning

Describe student's pre-injury behavior and attitudes within family setting.

_____

_____

_____

_____

_____

_____

_____

Describe student's pre-injury behavior within peer group in and out of school.

_____

_____

_____

_____

_____

_____

_____

_____

Describe

- *pre-injury employment*

_____

- *volunteer activities*

_____

- *extra-curricular activities*

_____

- *athletics and sports*

_____

- *special interests*

_____

6. Description of *Current* Functioning

Identification of the student's skills, knowledge, and abilities is essential to developing an educational plan. Start with listing the student's strengths in all categories. Then list the needs and barriers she/he faces.

Outline Levels	*(+) Strengths*	*(–) Needs/Barriers*
Cognitive-Communicative		

arousal/awareness
_____

attention/concentration (response to noise/activity)
_____

thinking and problem solving
_____

speed of thinking/responding
_____

written communication
_____

speech/language skills
_____

memory for new information
_____

thinking flexibility/response to change
_____

initiating/planning and follow-through
_____

sequencing/working through steps in a process
_____

ability to follow schedule
_____

ability to function independently:
in structured and unstructured settings
_____

ability to find way to/from and around school building
_____

physical/mental endurance
_____

other
_____

6. Description of Current Functioning *(continued)*

Outline Levels   *(+) Strengths*   *(–) Needs/Barriers*

Social/Behavioral

awareness of his/her of disability
_____

awareness of others
_____

awareness of social rules/roles
_____

self care/appearance/grooming
_____

age-appropriate behavior
_____

sexuality
_____

emotional expression/stability/depression
_____

use of alcohol/drugs
_____

other
_____

Sensorimotor

coordination and balance
_____

mobility
_____

handedness
_____

vision and hearing
_____

other
_____

6. Description of Current Functioning *(continued)*

Outline Levels   *(+) Strengths*   *(–) Needs/Barriers*

Academic

Current functioning in classroom/school environment

reading
_____

math
_____

written work
_____

other
_____

Program/structural modifications needed/required

schedules
_____

length of day
_____

need for structure
_____

frequent breaks
_____

location of instruction/classes
_____

length of assignments
_____

work expectations/speed
_____

test modifications
_____

instructional methods/materials/aids
_____

school staff
_____

adaptive equipment/techonology
_____

          Additional copies are available from the publisher.

6. Description of Current Functioning *(continued)*

Outline Levels   *(+) Strengths*   *(–) Needs/Barriers*

Program/structural modifications needed/required

organization systems _____

communication systems _____

behavior plans _____

peer support _____

motivation _____

reinforcers _____

7. Description of the Student's Goals
(as verbalized by the student)

The personal goals of the student (no matter what age) can be a powerful force leading to change and adaptation. Many times the goals appear to be completely unrealistic and unattainable. Sometimes the injury to the student's brain affects his/her judgment to the degree that she/he is unable to understand that a goal is not realistic. However, the goals can offer a clue to the student's interests and can be broken down into realistic steps.

Example

Tom is a high school student with a severe disability from a brain injury. In his junior year in high school, Tom was the star quarterback and planned to play football in college after graduation. Following his injury, he told the guidance counselor that he didn't need vocational counseling because he already knew what he was going to do. He would be the quarterback for the Detroit Lions professional football team. Clearly, this was not possible due to his cognitive and physical injuries. Tom's parents found his inability to recognize his physical limitations very distressing.

However, school staff focused on Tom's interest and worked with him to define the steps leading to his goal. Building his physical endurance through an exercise program, catching and throwing a ball, writing out and graphing football plays all worked to build important skills for Tom. As Tom made progress on his short term objectives, he began to become aware of how difficult it would be to attain his ultimate goal. Over time, he refocused his vocational goals on a more realistic job; a trainer in a health/fitness club.

7. Identify the student's short term goals as expressed by the student

short term — the next 3 to 6 months

Date: _____

_____

_____

_____

_____

_____

over the student's school career

_____

_____

_____

_____

_____

_____

long term — vocational, residential and community

_____

_____

_____

_____

_____

_____

8. Description of Parental/Family Support

family strengths/resources to cope

_____

_____

_____

insight into child's disability

_____

_____

_____

parental/family goals for student — short term; long term

_____

_____

_____

_____

parental concerns about return to school

_____

_____

_____

_____

family support services/training needed

_____

_____

_____

Notes

_____

_____

_____

_____

_____

_____

_____

_____

_____

_____

_____

_____

_____

_____

_____

_____

_____

_____

_____

_____

_____

_____

_____

Additional copies are available from the publisher.

Transition Planning Worksheet

Moving to the Next Grade

by Gary F. Wolcott, M.Ed.

Parents Say	"Every September I feel like we have to start over again — things that helped my child in school last year have to be worked out again." or "I sometimes worry that because she is new to the school this year they won't know what to do if the problem comes up again."
Teachers Say	"It's a real challenge to get to know each child and their unique needs within the first few weeks of school."

These are common concerns for parents and teachers, at the beginning of the school year. However, they are even greater concerns for a student with a brain injury. The educational needs of this student are more complex due to a broad range of learning, behavioral, and physical problems.

Each school district has a procedure for passing student information to the educators working at the next grade level. This worksheet is intended to support and supplement such procedures. Since educational programs for the student with a brain injury require close coordination and support in the school environment, this worksheet defines the basic information teachers and other school staff need to start the new school year.

This worksheet can be filled out by either parents or teachers. Often it has been helpful to both because it summarizes the student's needs and identifies the location of assessments, plans, and specialists who have worked with the student.

Date:
Student Name:
Age/Grade Now:　　　　　　　　**Age/Grade at Time of Injury:**

1. Current Educational Plan & Quarterly Reports (from last school year)

List Reports　　　　　　　　　　　　　　　　　*Dates of Reports*

_____

_____

_____

_____

_____

_____

_____

_____

_____

_____

2. School Work

Work samples
List Samples Attached   *Description*

_____

_____

_____

Books and materials used
List

_____

_____

_____

Behavior management techniques
List   *Explanation*   *Reinforcers/Consequences*

_____

_____

_____

Adaptive/assistive equipment or interventions
List

_____

_____

_____

Learning style/general strengths and needs
List

_____

_____

_____

3. Current Medical Summary

Brief history of injury/illness and medical treatment

_____

_____

_____

_____

_____

_____

Current medications & purpose

_____

_____

_____

_____

_____

Medical issues at school

List issue	*Explanation*	*Methods of response*

Additional copies are available from the publisher.

4. Special Services Summary

Service	Date of most recent assessment	Summary of Recommendations
Psychology/Neuropsychology		
Physical Therapy		
Occupational Therapy		
Speech/Language Therapy		
Adaptive Physical Education		
Other		

5. List of Important Participants or Contacts

Name	Address	Phone	Role
1.			
2.			
3.			
4.			
5.			
6.			

Notes

_____

_____

_____

_____

_____

_____

_____

_____

_____

_____

_____

_____

_____

_____

_____

_____

_____

_____

_____

_____

_____

Transition Planning Worksheet

Moving between Classes in Middle or High School

by Gary F. Wolcott, M.Ed.

Parents Say: "I'm worried about my child going into middle school. We've come so far since the injury and worked out lots of support in elementary school. But so much more is expected academically in middle school with a lot more responsibility on the student to get the work done."
or
"The academic part of high school is hard for my son but he's managing. Where he gets into trouble is the little stuff; being on-time, remembering to bring the right books to class, getting anxious about doing something new."

Teachers Say: "Most kids this age are disorganized but can 'get it together' when pushed. But the student with a brain injury never seems to be able to work it out and usually gets worse under pressure."

Principals Say: "Its tough to communicate every detail of the education plan to all of the staff involved. Sometimes things don't go smoothly."

Each student entering middle school and high school faces a significant organizational challenge in adjusting to many teachers, moving between classes, and managing long and short term assignments in numerous courses. But these organizational problems are

Common responses are:

"He's acting like all other junior high students"

or

"How do we know it's not just adolescent behavior?"

These do not accurately identify the cause of the problems.

even more difficult for a student with a brain injury. Learning and remembering how to get around a new school building, what time classes change, what class or activity comes next, or the locker combination, can easily overwhelm this student. Add to these tasks the physical and mental fatigue that accompanies recovery from a brain injury and it is clear that the middle or high school student is facing a great challenge.

It is critical that a support system be developed to help the student adjust and succeed in middle school or high school. This support system must:

1) be coordinated among all school personnel who supervise the student (teachers, guidance counselors, and aides);

2) provide adequate support and strategies for the student to do his school work in a way that appears as normal to his peers as possible;

3) be understood and accepted by the student.

Since educational programs for the student with a brain injury require close coordination and support in the school environment, this worksheet can provide a blueprint for planning around key issues. This worksheet can be filled out in a meeting with the student, parents, teachers and other staff. A backup plan is included in the worksheet. It is important to recognize that situations will come up that can't be anticipated. Steps are listed to help the student "get back on track." When all can agree, the worksheet is signed and circulated to all school staff who come in contact with the student.

Date:	
Student Name:	
Age/Grade Now:	Age/Grade at Time of Injury:

1. Summary of Student's Challenges

Issue	Location	Time of Day	Other Persons Involved
1)			
2)			
3)			
4)			
5)			

2. Transition Issues to Address

Finding way to class (spatial orientation)

Adaptive Strategy	*Staff Person to Monitor*

Time to move between classes (ample time to get from place to place)

Adaptive Strategy	*Staff Person to Monitor*

Following schedule (in the right place at the right time)
Adaptive Strategy   *Staff Person to Monitor*

_____

_____

_____

_____

Time to finish tests/quizzes or other classroom work
(adequate time to get work done due to slowed speed of thinking and working)
Adaptive Strategy   *Staff Person to Monitor*

_____

_____

_____

_____

Managing books/materials (moving, storing, and having books)
Adaptive Strategy   *Staff Person to Monitor*

_____

_____

_____

_____

Managing homework assignments
Adaptive Strategy   *Staff Person to Monitor*

_____

_____

_____

_____

Learning Problems (reading disability,inabiliity to express ideas in writing)
Adaptive Strategy   *Staff Person to Monitor*

_____

_____

_____

_____

3. If These Adaptive Strategies Don't Work *(a backup plan)*

Procedure to follow   **Staff Person Responsible**

1) _____

_____

_____

2) _____

_____

_____

3) _____

_____

_____

4. Next Meeting to Evaluate this Plan

Date, Time, & Location of Meeting   **Staff Person Responsible**

_____

_____

5. Acknowledgement and Agreement by All Participants

	Name	Signature	Date
Student			
Student's Parent(s)			
Home Room Teacher			
Guidance Counselor			
Physical Education Teacher			
Teacher:			
Teacher:			
Teacher:			
Aide:			
Lunch Room Aide(s)			
Therapists (e.g., speech, OT, PT)			
Principal/Director of Special Education			

Further Reading

When your child is seriously injured: The emotional impact on families
by Marilyn Lash, M.S.W. 1991.
Published by EXCEPTIONAL PARENT, Department ML,
P.O. Box 8045, Brick, NJ 08723
Credit card orders: (800) 535-1910. (Price: $4.50)

When your child goes to school after an injury
by Marilyn Lash, M.S.W. 1992.
Published by EXCEPTIONAL PARENT, Department ML,
P.O. Box 8045, Brick, NJ 08723
Credit card orders: (800) 535-1910. (Price: $7.50)

When young children are injured:
Families as caregivers in hospitals and at home
by Jane Haltiwanger, M.A., and Marilyn Lash, M.S.W. 1994.
Published by EXCEPTIONAL PARENT, Department ML,
P.O. Box 8045, Brick, NJ 08723
Credit card orders: (800) 535-1910. (Price: $7.50)

Educational Dimensions of Acquired Brain Injury
edited by Ronald C. Savage, Ed.D. and Gary F. Wolcott, M.Ed. 1994.
PRO-Ed, 8700 Shoal Creek Blvd, Austin, TX 78757-6897
(512) 451-3246 (Price $39.00)

Head Injury: A Family Matter
by Janet M. Williams and Thomas Kay. 1991.
Paul Brookes Publishing Company
P.O. Box 10624, Baltimore, MD 21285-0624
Tel (410) 337-9580 (Price: $30.00)

Head Injury in Children and Adolescents:
A Resource for School and Allied Professionals
by Vivian Begali, M.Ed., Ed.S. Second edition, 1993.
Clinical Psychology Publishing Co., Inc.
4 Conant Square, Brandon, Vermont 05733.
Tel. (800) 433-8234.

Pediatric Traumatic Brain Injury: Proactive Intervention
Jean Blosser, Ed.D. and Roberta DePompei, Ph.D. 1994.
Published by Singular Publishing Group, Inc.
4284 41st St., San Diego, CA 92105-1197 (Price $39.50)

Psychological Management of Traumatic Brain Injuries
in Children & Adolescents
by Ellen Lehr, Ph.D. 1990
Aspen Publishers, Inc. P.O. Box 990, Frederick, MD 21701.
(800) 234-1660 (Price $57.00)

Traumatic Head Injury in Children and Adolescents:
A Sourcebook for Teachers and Other School Personnel
by Mary P. Mira, Bonnie Tucker and Janet S. Tyler. 1992.
PRO-Ed, 8700 Shoal Creek Blvd, Austin, TX 78757-6897
(512) 451-3246 (Price $19.00)

An Educator's Manual: A Teacher's Guide to Students
with Brain Injuries
edited by Ron Savage, Ed.D. and Gary Wolcott, M.Ed. 1995.
National Head Injury Foundation, 1776 Massachusetts Avenue,
Suite 100, Washington, DC 20036-1914
(202) 643-6443 (Call for Price)

Resources

Research and Training Center in Rehabilitation and Childhood Trauma
Department of Physical Medicine and Rehabilitation
New England Medical Center and Tufts University School of Medicine
750 Washington St., #75 K-R, Boston, MA 02111-1901,
Telephone Voice and TT (617) 636-5031

National Head Injury Foundation (NHIF)
1776 Massachusetts Avenue, Washington, DC 20036
Telephone: Voice (202) 296-6443
Ask for the address and telephone number of your State chapter of NHIF

National Information Center for Children and Youth with Disabilities (NICHCY)
P.O. Box 1492, Washington, DC 20013
Telephone: Voice: (800) 999-5599; TT: (703) 893-8614